Kid Culture

Children & Adults
& Popular Culture

KID CULTURE

CHILDREN & ADULTS
& POPULAR CULTURE

by

KATHLEEN McDONNELL

SECOND STORY *Press*

CANADIAN CATALOGUING IN PUBLICATION DATA

McDonnell, Kathleen, 1947 -
Kid Culture: children & adults & popular culture

Includes bibliographical references.
ISBN 0-929005-64-3

1. Children – Social life and customs. 2. Popular culture. I. Title.

HQ781.M33 1994   305.23   C94-932386-1

Cover Art by Barbara Klunder
Edited by Wendy Thomas
Printed and Bound in Canada

*Second Story Press gratefully acknowledges the assistance of
the Ontario Arts Council and The Canada Council*

Published by
SECOND STORY PRESS
720 Bathurst Street Suite 301
Toronto, Ontario
M5S 2R4

Contents

Acknowledgments

This book consists of my own observations, thoughts and (in the opinion of some) cockamamie theories, but these are grounded in the stimulating and delightful connections I've made with numerous children over the past few years. I can't name them all, but I can say a heartfelt thank you.

My own children are probably a bit tired of being thanked by now, and one of these days they're liable to rise up and refuse to go on serving as my in-house laboratory. In the meantime, once again, thanks to Martha and Ivy Farquhar-McDonnell and their many friends, from whom I've learned and keep learning.

Thanks also to the students and teachers at Downtown Alternative School, Island Public School and Jesse Ketchum School, who welcomed me into their classrooms.

Various friends served as sounding boards and shared their own ideas as I worked on this book; chief among them were Alec Farquhar and Ann Lacey. Esther Fine showed me the draft of her thesis, which was a great help at the beginning stages of my research. Anita Sheth shared some insightful thoughts on television and introduced me to the work of John Fiske, for which I'm extremely grateful.

Anne Rochon Ford, Bill Elleker and Liz Martin took time out of their busy schedules to read the manuscript and give me their unfailingly helpful comments.

I also want to thank the Canada Council and the Ontario Arts Council for financial support, as well as Margie Wolfe, Bill Elleker, Michele Landsberg and Pierre Tetrault for their letters of support.

Wendy Thomas waded into my sometimes meandering prose and helped me focus, clarify and streamline. Many thanks.

I'm grateful to the fine women of Second Story Press, who've been so supportive of my work over the years.

CHAPTER ONE

The War with No Winners, or How I Learned to Stop Worrying and Trust the Kids

POPULAR CULTURE is an all-pervasive fact of modern life. We've heard tales of Amazon villages or remote Arctic outposts where the Rolling Stones blare on radios, where evening storytelling has been abandoned in favour of "Dallas" and "Bonanza" reruns, where TV has virtually, in the words of one tribal elder, "stolen the night." Wherever it rears its many-faceted head, popular culture asserts an instant domination over existing traditions, creating new markets and undreamt-of desires.

But you don't have to go to the Amazon or the high Arctic to see the irresistible lure of pop culture in action. It's there in plain view in the daily lives of North American kids. Like tribal peoples, kids also gravitate on contact to pop culture forms, almost invariably choosing (when they're given a choice) television over a book, high-concept commercial toys over traditional ones, cartoons over "educational" programs. Pop culture has become a kind of common currency among children, an adhesive that binds them together in a subculture of their own — one that is becoming increasingly global in scale.

Adults, particularly educated, middle-class adults, are becoming ever more alarmed about pop culture's grip on childhood. Over the past decade, more and more parents have become engaged in a kind of cultural warfare with their children. In households across North America, battles of will rage over sex-stereotyped toys, over violent films and TV programs, over video-game addiction. Sometimes the parents win a round; sometimes the kids come out on top. But it's a war with no winners, one nobody feels very good about, one in which each side feels misunderstood by the other.

Parents fear that popular culture is poisoning kids' minds, producing violence-prone sons and passive, appearance-obsessed daughters. In the eyes of many adults, pop culture has come to be viewed as the pornography of childhood, an almost demonic force in modern life. The result is that wide swaths of children's culture are being condemned wholesale, as parents take their concerns into the political arena and call for curbs or outright bans on war toys, sexually suggestive rock lyrics and violent TV programs.

For their part, kids are wondering what all the fuss is about. They are genuinely mystified by the openly contemptuous attitude so many adults have towards the very things they like the most. "We're only playing," they object, frustrated that adults just don't seem to understand the distinction (which seems crystal clear to them) between doing and pretending, between reality and fantasy. For many kids, the controversy just adds up to familiar, typical adult behaviour — forever butting into kids' lives, trying to control their every waking moment, and just generally spoiling their fun. It's an old story, this power struggle between the generations. The sixties even coined a term for it: "the generation gap." But what distinguishes this latest phase of the generation wars is the omnipresent influence of popular culture. Never before have kids had access to such a vast array of entertainments, nor have they been the target market of an enormous multi-billion-dollar industry aimed specifically at them.

I come by my stripes in the pop culture wars honestly. A decade ago, in those halcyon days B.C. — before children — I fully expected that my household would be a model of progressive values, a haven from the violence, racism, sexism and consumerism that seemed rampant in society at large. No toys that transgressed those values would be allowed to cross our threshold. No offending television programs would appear on our screen. Why, maybe we'd just get rid of the TV altogether. And if they — our children-to-be — didn't like it, well, too bad. Just who was running this show, anyway? Wasn't it our job as parents to mould them in our own leftist-feminist image, to shield them from the pernicious influences of patriarchy and capitalism? Of course, I had yet to come face to face with the awesome force of nature that is a young child's will. Nor had I taken into account the incredible staying power of a certain 12-inch-high blonde.

It was around the age of four that our first child, Martha, began to lobby for a Barbie doll. When we refused outright, she took strong issue with us, and why not? We'd raised her to be assertive, to question authority. Just what was the problem, Martha demanded to know. Was Barbie too expensive? Not really, we had to admit. Unless you get into expensive accessories like RVs and Malibu beach houses, Barbie fit comfortably in the range of affordable toys. Well, then, would she break easily like the other cheaply made "hunk of junk" toys we were always complaining about? Probably not. Was having a Barbie doll some kind of safety hazard, then? These were objections Martha may not have liked, but they were at least familiar and understandable. But she couldn't have Barbie because she was pretty? Because she wore nice clothes? Because she was "sexist," whatever that was? What kind of cockamamie adult reasoning were we trying to foist on her this time?

I honestly can't recall exactly how or when we first caved in, but I do remember that Martha's first Barbie was second-hand, so at least we weren't purchasing one ourselves and giving support to the Barbie industry. She was blonde, of course, and bizarrely proportioned, with feet moulded to fit high-heeled shoes and a head of hair that looked like it might account for two-thirds of her body weight. We didn't realize it then, but there was no turning back; Barbie had gained a spike-heeled foothold in our house, and from there it was the proverbial slippery slope. More hand-me-downs found their way into the house, followed, in time, by brand-new Barbies — Skating Star Barbie one Christmas, Summer Fun Barbie, complete with neon bikini and hot pink sailboat, the next. For a woman who had once vowed "Barbie? Over my dead body!", my main problem now was to keep from tripping over the piles of Barbies, in varying states of undress, that littered the floor of our house.

My mate and I adopted a strategy of sorts, what I've come to think of as the Sneer Tactic. We figured one way to assuage our guilt at having caved in was to ensure that Martha got as little enjoyment out of her Barbies as possible. Whenever she got them out, she could count on hearing a lecture from one of us on some aspect of sex-role stereotyping. Over time, these lectures gradually degenerated into a predictable stream of snide comments about Barbie. I can still recall my shock when, one day, she turned on me in fury and said, "I don't make fun of the things you like! You always talk about respecting other people's opinions. But you don't respect mine!" Caught — not for the first time — with my ideological pants down, I had to admit she had a point. Now it was I who was confused. To grudgingly allow Barbie into the house was one thing. Did my principles now demand that I respect her, too — or at least Martha's view of her?

I looked around at the other parents I knew and saw we were all in the same boat. All of us were engaged in similar battles with our kids, and none of it seemed to be working. Our daughters were all preoccupied with wearing dresses, make-up, high-heeled shoes. Our sons were all caught up with toy trucks, guns, Star Wars and GI Joe paraphernalia. We kept coming up against the irritating but inescapable fact that our kids truly, passionately liked all this stuff we considered so politically retrograde.

One day Martha and her friend Carla emerged from the bedroom holding a couple of naked Barbies above their heads. They started marching around the living room, giggling and chanting the word "scaaaarrry" over and over in a sing-song. Closer inspection revealed that the Barbies were not only naked, but that their bodies had been streaked with black Magic Marker. Also, one Barbie was missing her head altogether. These Barbies had been re-christened, the girls informed me. Henceforth they would be known as Stinky-Bum Barbie and Dirty-Bum Barbie.

I wasn't sure how to react. Was this strange ritual evidence of how thoroughly their minds had already been polluted by misogynist culture? Should I give them a lecture on the beauty of the female body? Or were they just playing around with the idea of being bad, thumbing their noses at the pristine, pastel world of the Barbie ads? Whichever it was, it seemed to me a good sign that they felt free to put Barbie in whatever outlandish scenarios they could imagine her. And they were certainly having a good time doing it. Recasting Barbie as her own wild, stinky, dirty shadow may have been "scaaarry" but to them it was hysterically funny at the same time.

After that incident, I began to notice other ways in which Martha and her friends departed from the script set out in the Barbie ads. We adults think Barbie's world is all about Ken and dating, for instance. But in the homes of all the girls I knew, Ken was nowhere to be found. The girls, and the Barbies, seemed to get along just fine without him. Their

Barbie universe was an all-female one, and in their play they spun out stories that focused almost exclusively on girls — what they do together, their bonds with each other. It began to dawn on me that Barbie may not entirely deserve the bad rap we feminists had pinned on her. Maybe she was serving as a vehicle for some "girl-positive" ideas. Maybe, viewed from a certain perspective, she was even a closet feminist.

So I tried to stop judging so much and began to simply observe my kids and their friends at play. I started watching TV with them and talked with them about what they liked and why. As I learned to listen better and to take their reactions and opinions seriously, I more and more found myself questioning many of the assumptions that I, and most of the other adults I knew, had long held about popular culture. Was it really so unredeemably bad for kids? How could we be so sure? We were awfully quick with our snap judgements of programs we'd never bothered to watch, awfully ready to ban certain toys without paying much attention to how our kids actually played with them. I decided to try to find out for myself just what was it about these shows, these toys that made kids gravitate to them so strongly, in the face of such vehement adult disapproval. Were they simply dupes of marketing ploys, robots brainwashed by consumerism, as we believed? Or was there more to it? Could there be aspects of popular culture that met some deeper need for kids?

Feeling a bit like an anthropologist in an alien world, I embarked on a nearly decade-long odyssey, trying to get a handle on this modern phenomenon of Kid Culture. I watched kids' TV shows. I went to kids' feature films. I may be the only adult in North America who sat through the first two Teenage Mutant Ninja Turtle movies taking notes in the dark. I re-acquainted myself with Archie comics and *Mad* magazine. I even made a half-hearted foray into the world of computer games, at which I proved to be a dismal failure — I could never get past the first exploding turtle in Super Mario

Land. Though it's mildly embarrassing to admit it, I found I actually enjoyed much of what I saw, and I suspect many other adults do, too. There is something in children's entertainments that makes them relatively easy to sit through, which I gradually came to realize was the simple pleasure of narrative, of storytelling. Popular culture has in fact become the modern repository of narrative, the place where the idea of "story" still reigns supreme, while in the realm of high culture it has come to be seen as old-fashioned and sentimental. Kids' popular culture has a particularly strong grounding in narrative because kids themselves demand it. They have an endless appetite for stories: It's their main way of interacting with and making sense of the world, a subject I'll be exploring more fully in subsequent chapters.

Of course, one person can't hope to get more than a fragmentary grasp on the vast landscape of pop culture for children. I decided that the best I could realistically do was to let myself be guided by my own and my kids' tastes and interests, which has inevitably given a certain slant to the content of this book. Since both my children are girls and my own interests are female-centred, I've given considerably more attention here to girls' play, stories and preoccupations than I have to boys'. Since female culture generally gets short shrift in our society, I see this aspect of the book as simply a modest step towards righting this historical imbalance. But it also means that certain areas that are more in the domain of boys, especially computer and video games, don't command as much attention here as their importance in contemporary Kid Culture actually warrants.

Reading kids' original stories has provided me with another window into Kid Culture. In doing storywriting projects with children in some downtown Toronto schools over the past few years, I've been struck by the strong gender differences in the stories kids write. The ones I've read by girls are typically about friendship and fairy princesses and talking animals. Boys' stories, on the other hand, are usually full of blood and gore, fighting and death, good guys and bad guys. When I first encountered these stories by boys, I was troubled by all the violence and wondered how to respond to it. But I was also thrown off guard by the fact that these violence-drenched tales were written by sweet-faced, friendly boys who didn't strike me as being on the road to becoming serial killers or wife beaters. Still, I felt it was my duty to register at least some disapproval, to let them know that violence was unacceptable and encourage them to find other things to write about. But it became clear to me that even had they agreed to try to write "nicer" stories to please me, they probably wouldn't have known where to begin. Action stories — variations on the male quest tale — were the only type of story the boys seemed to be interested in. Fighting, slaying enemies with complicated weaponry — all this was, for them, part and parcel of the action genre. In asking them to take out the violence, I might as well have told them to throw their entire output of stories out the window.

I gradually came to see that there was more going on in the boys' stories than just a mindless revelling in violence for its own sake. I remember one story in particular that shifted my thinking. An eight-year-old boy wrote about a pilot named Zack (who, he specified, flew an "SR-71 Blackbird") who gets shot down in the jungle. He's found by some "Indians" who try to take him prisoner but he manages to scare them off with his gun. Zack later witnesses some members of his own air force — who are "Americans" — killing the Indians for no reason, and at that moment decides to turn against them and fight on the Indians' side. The rest of the story was a gory litany of pitched battles, ambushes, shootings and killings, with Zack and his new allies emerging, of course, victorious. The story closes with Zack living "happily ever after with the Indians." What struck me about this story was that, for all the fighting and bloodshed, there was something else going on that I would have missed if I'd dismissed it as a simple regurgitation of all the violent action films this boy had obviously seen. It seemed to me that the story was an attempt to grapple with the whole notion of "us" and "them," of good guys and bad guys. In the story, the hero undergoes the shattering experience of realizing that his own people, his "tribe," are evil and abusive, and he takes the extraordinary step of going over to the other side. It seemed likely to me that the boy who wrote the story had been influenced by the movie *Dances with Wolves,* which came out around that time and featured a similar storyline about a soldier who "goes native." But it was clearly a story he wanted to tell and reflected some questions he was trying to answer for himself about violence and the dilemma of war: Just who are the good guys and who are the bad guys? If "our" side is good, then why do we kill people?

Meanwhile, though the girls didn't exhibit anything like the same penchant for action and violence in their stories, I noticed that they, too, often wrote versions of the male quest tale. That is, their stories were frequently built around male protagonists, and it was more often the male characters who got to have what adventures there were to be had. I began to see that both the boys' and the girls' stories were, in their respective ways, reflecting the preponderance of male-centred stories and the corresponding dearth of female-centred stories in our culture. This "gender gap" in stories, and how it's being perpetuated as well as rectified in popular culture, is a major theme of this book.

Reading kids' stories and talking to them about their work became another tool to help me understand how kids both use and are influenced by pop culture narratives. Right from the beginning I was struck by the energy and exuberance, the strong storytelling impulse at work in the stories I read by these inner-city kids. To my way of thinking, they didn't at all fit the stereotype of the unimaginative couch potatoes and video-zombies TV culture is supposed to have created. Though the kids' stories I've seen are typically shot through with references to video games, characters from TV shows, and storylines from hit movies, they don't just parrot what they see but use it in their own ways. I've rarely come across a kid's story that hasn't had at least some evidence of a creative stamp, a personal voice at work. And they're just as likely to draw from sources other than pop culture for inspiration — fairy tales, well-known works of children's literature, the bits and pieces they know of classical mythology. I've been continually fascinated by the ingenious ways children mix and match elements from wildly different sources to graft together sometimes startlingly original concoctions. Like true writers everywhere, they create their own syntheses — sending Ninja Turtles into battle against Minotaurs, and fairy queens shopping at the local mall. One reason for this is that they haven't yet learned to make the distinction — so important to adults — between high and low culture: they embrace it all, equally.

I began to see that, like Martha with her Barbies, these kids were not merely the passive receptacles of pop culture, but active spectators and participants in creating their own version of it. It seemed to me what they were trying to do, in their free-wheeling, eclectic way, was to cobble together a mythology they could claim as their own, a mythology for which the much-maligned popular culture provided major source material. The work of John Fiske, some of whose ideas I'll be discussing later, helped crystallize these insights and provided a broader theoretical framework for them.

I think it's time we called a truce in this thankless, no-win war with our kids over pop culture. This doesn't mean putting aside our concerns or turning a blind eye to its excesses. Nor does it mean throwing up our hands, abdicating our legitimate responsibilities as adults and giving kids carte blanche to watch and do whatever they want. But it does mean engaging in genuine dialogue with kids and making an effort to find some kind of *modus vivendi* with Kid Culture. In truth, we don't really have much choice: popular culture is a fact of contemporary life that isn't going to go away. The only way to avoid it is to go live in the woods or on another planet, and even then, the kids will find a way to build a satellite dish.

Kids crave the menu pop culture has to offer, and it's up to adults to try to discover why this is. Even addiction bespeaks a truer hunger. What looks like nothing but toxic junk food to us may be meeting some deeper need for them. XUXA is a case in point. The phenomenally popular Brazilian children's entertainer has a four-hour daily TV show, a shorter version of which premiered on North American TV in 1993. XUXA's go-go dancer persona and the show's anarchic, carnival atmosphere have led critics to denounce it as a vulgar, thoroughly commercialized electronic babysitter. But in a country with thousands of abandoned, homeless children, XUXA may be responding to a need that the present social structures in Brazil can't fulfil. No wonder one Brazilian anthropologist called her "a modern-day Virgin Mary" and an "exalted fairy godmother whose presence transforms everything to happiness and beauty in a child's life."

It's true, of course, that children are not a critical audience in the same sense adults are. But neither are they mere dupes and robots blindly following the dictates of the pop culture moguls, as so many adults maintain. Personally, I've developed a healthy respect for kids' instincts. If they like something, particularly if a lot of them like something, there's a reason for it. There's something there, even if it's not readily apparent to adult eyes. I don't want to suggest that commercial manipulation isn't a factor in pop culture's appeal, only that it has other dimensions as well. Kids watching a Disney film or a TV cartoon may not be aware that what they're seeing is a product produced for profit by a multi-billion-dollar industry. They're experiencing it as narrative, as entertainment.

Though I think it's important to make kids aware of pop culture's economic clout and help them develop a critical sense about the values that go along with it, my primary focus in this book is on how kids interact with the narratives of popular culture. Movies, television, cartoons are all indisputably commercial products, but they are also significant expressions of a cultural ethos.

I come neither to praise popular culture — the industry itself does that particular job just fine — nor to bury it, but to understand it as the complex, peculiarly modern phenomenon that it is. There's no doubt that pop culture reinforces some of the most regressive aspects of modern life. But at its best it offers a window for new images, new possibilities, new ways of seeing. Of course, most of it falls between these two extremes — neither so dangerous nor so full of promise. But I think that to some extent we have to put up with one to get the other. Pop culture operates a bit like the id, the unconscious of the larger culture. There's beauty and garbage, fresh visions and exhausted old patterns all mixed in together.

I think we can make pop culture work for us. But we can do that only if we learn to do more than just censor and rage against it. Rather, we have to try to understand and even embrace its wild, anarchic character. We also have to come to grips with the fact that Kid Culture belongs to kids themselves. We adults just don't get it. Having left childhood behind, we're mostly aliens in that world. We don't speak the language. We don't see things the same way. The generation gap is, in a very real sense, a cultural gap.

CHAPTER TWO

The Contours of Kid Culture

NOT LONG AGO I took note of a newspaper column by philosophy professor Thomas Hurka that examined the question of children's rights. In it, Professor Hurka argues that children have a right to autonomy, but only to "the autonomy they will exercise in the future," once they become adults. He goes on to list a number of rights that belong to children: the right to be educated, the right to an "open future" with many options. But what struck me was that none of the rights he listed applied to childhood itself, to the here-and-now of children's lives. They would kick in only once the superior state of adulthood had been achieved. In Professor Hurka's scheme of things, children's present holds little validity or interest — only their future does. In a sense, childhood doesn't really exist in its own right. Its only value is as a training ground for adulthood.

Unfortunately, Professor Hurka's column expresses a fairly common set of adult attitudes towards childhood. His stated interest is in children's welfare, but the whole thrust of his argument subtly devalues the state of childhood itself. Since children are in a sense unfinished products and have not yet achieved the "goal" of maturity, their lives are somehow considered trivial, not deserving of our interest or attention. Underlying this attitude, I believe, is an adult version of the developmental disdain children typically feel for the stages of life they've already passed through.* An older child tends to look down on a younger sibling who still wears diapers, believes in Santa Claus or plays with dolls. It's perfectly normal for children to feel this way; it's partly what gives them incentive to master each new level of development. But we supposedly mature adults should have grown out of developmental disdain, the need to convince ourselves that we are superior, more highly evolved beings.

The real shame is that adults have no idea what we're missing by regarding children in this way. The world of childhood is vastly more interesting when viewed on its own terms than as merely a series of "developmental tasks," a way station on the road to adulthood. Anthropologist Ashley Montagu's view of childhood differs sharply from Hurka's, for example. In his book *Growing Young*, Montagu takes strong issue with the common view that achieving adulthood is the goal of life. Rather than hurrying children to become like adults, he maintains that they should be encouraged to retain their so-called childish traits, such as playfulness, emotional directness and openness to new things, for as long as possible. Moreover, Montagu argues, adults should strive to be more like children rather than the other way around! In his view, our life's task should be to grow young rather than to grow old, to honour childhood rather than devalue it.

In this chapter I want to look at childhood as an entity in its own right, by examining it as a culture with its own particular sensibilities and preoccupations, its own sense of humour and ways of seeing the world. I'll also try to show how contemporary childhood is being indelibly shaped by the popular media, creating the peculiarly modern phenomenon of Kid Culture. Viewing childhood as a culture can be enormously helpful to our understanding of why adults and kids regard popular culture so differently. It helps explain why adults,

---

* I thank my friend Bill Elleker for giving a name to this phenomenon and calling my attention to it.

with the best intentions and the most progressive sentiments, have had so little impact on kids' tastes. In my view, a culture is not just a set of fairly superficial "attitudes" but a vital, complex entity, a constellation of beliefs and behaviours deeply rooted in the collective history and personal psyches of its members. I find it interesting that the very word "culture" has both sociological and biological meanings, because in some ways cultures act almost like "organic" entities — unpredictable, in constant flux, strongly resistant to outside control.

THE IDEA OF CHILDHOOD

Childhood not only has its own culture; it has a history of its own as well. Childhood as a biological phase of human development has, of course, always existed. But the idea of childhood as a stage of life and as an entity distinct from adulthood is largely a modern phenomenon. Adults and children didn't always live in such separate spheres as they do in modern industrial societies. The French cultural historian Philippe Ariès argues in his classic work *Centuries of Childhood* that the idea of childhood as a distinct stage of life with its own particular character has emerged only over the past couple of centuries of Western civilization. Before the Industrial Revolution and the modern era, children were considered part of the adult world as soon as they were no longer infants. They were depicted in medieval and Renaissance paintings as pint-size grown-ups, and their style of dress was indistinguishable from that of adults. Ariès notes that portraits of children doing childlike activities like playing games began to be commonplace only around the seventeenth century in Europe. At that time, a particular childhood costume with more precious qualities that set it apart from adults' style of dress also appeared on the scene. These developments, Ariès argues, signal that the idea of childhood consciousness. By the early eighteenth century, children had become fully established as subjects for contemplation, discussion and artistic depiction in their own right. This period saw the emerging idealization of childhood, which began with Rousseau and the Romantics and which reached its zenith (or nadir, depending on your point of view) in the sentimental stories and illustrations of the Victorian era in England.

The beginning of the modern era in the late nineteenth and early twentieth centuries saw the emergence of a new class of experts — educators, doctors and behavioural theorists with a professional interest in children. Childhood had finally become an object of real adult interest and thus of serious study. In the work of Piaget and Freud, the everyday lives of children take centre stage, at least insofar as they provide the raw material out of which the adult would be moulded. Piaget's radical contribution was to base his theories of child development on direct and detailed observation of children's actual behaviour. He was interested in how children really are rather than how adults thought they should be. At the turn of the century, Freud's theory of childhood sexuality exploded the whole notion of children's innocence. Freudianism may have restored some necessary balance to the rampant sentimentalization, but it also revived the more archaic notion of children's inherent evilness, which the Victorian era had for a time driven underground. But whatever else one might say about Freud and his followers, their importance to the history of childhood lies in the fact that, like Piaget, they took childhood seriously. They gave far more attention to the events of childhood, and far more importance to children's thoughts and feelings, than any generation of adults before them.

Even earlier, the eighteenth century saw the emergence of a related phenomenon: the voice of the child begins to be heard. In the beginning, of course, children did not actually speak for themselves in the public arena. But they did find an eloquent spokesperson in the form of the poet and artist William Blake. Blake's *Songs of Innocence* and *Songs of*

Experience show a deep identification with children and an understanding of their mentality rarely seen before. He was one of the first adults to adopt without irony or embarrassment the voice and perspective of the child: "I have no name: I am but two days old," he writes in "Infant Joy." Blake was also a passionate advocate for children. Much of his work was fueled by outrage at the exploitive child labour practices of the early Industrial Revolution, and by his belief that much of what we have come to call "maturity" is actually the result of stifling children's essential spirit and vitality.

Childhood may have emerged as a separate realm in modern times, but how accurate is it to describe it as having a culture of its own? One of the fundamental characteristics of a culture is its ability to transmit its values and behaviours to succeeding generations. While adults may be the ones who teach children arithmetic, manners and morals, it is other children who initiate them into the world of childhood, who instruct them in the fundamentals of how to be a kid, which is of far more pressing interest to them than arithmetic, manners and morals. This cultural transmission, which begins virtually at birth, goes largely unnoticed by adults. This is partly because much of it goes on almost in secret. As much as possible, kids like to do their important business away from prying adult eyes. But adults also tend to ignore this secret life because it undermines one of our most cherished illusions — that we are the centre of our children's universe. Just watch a couple of new parents bask in their newborn's adoring gaze, then notice what happens when an older child enters the picture. The baby's attention invariably shifts to the other child's face, voice, behaviour. For the adults, it's the first in a lifetime of reminders that, by and large, kids much prefer the company of other kids. Their own world, in which we are outsiders, is much more interesting to them than ours.

Though much of this cultural initiation into childhood happens within the family, carried out by older siblings, it reaches a whole other level when children start day care or school. Adults think day care is for supervision and that school is for learning knowledge and skills. But kids have a different view. For them, the primary importance of these institutions is social. These are the places they come together in groups, to form bonds outside their families and to create, transmit and perpetuate their own culture. It bothers adults that the social aspects of school seem to be so much more important to kids than academics. What we fail to realize is the extent to which kids use these bonds and the intensely social world around them to make the often stultifying, de-energizing experience of being "schooled" more bearable.

Children are not only adept at handing down their own culture. They are also responsible for keeping whole segments of the wider culture alive. Folklorists such as Edith Fowke and Iona and Peter Opie have published extensive collections of children's songs, games and playground chants. Fowke's book *Sally Go Round the Sun* documents what she calls "the folk poetry of childhood" and demonstrates kids' tenacity at keeping these folk traditions alive, transmitting them from generation to generation over extraordinary periods of time. Many of the rhymes and circle games in the Opies' *The Singing Game* are centuries old. The most ancient of them, such as "The Mulberry Bush" and its variant "Nuts in May," are descended from circle dances and songs that were formerly adult pastimes. This is an interesting point that underscores Ariès's contention that leisure activities in former times typically crossed generational lines, often including the whole community, young and old alike. That is, earlier generations didn't share our modern sharp distinction between "adult" and "children's" entertainment. As certain pastimes such as circle dances fell out of fashion with adults, they were picked up and kept alive by children. According to Ariès, this explains why medieval society strikes us as somewhat "puerile" today: to us they appear to be acting like children.

Six- to ten-year-old girls are the chief guardians of this centuries-old culture. Their elaborate hand-clapping games, skipping songs, magic spells and other rhymes constitute an entirely oral culture that is passed down through generations of playground activity. But like any true culture, the forms they use are not static, but constantly evolving and incorporating elements from the present. The Opies list girls' songs and clapping rhymes from the past few decades that contain mentions of film stars Shirley Temple, Betty Grable, Diana Dors, Marilyn Monroe and J.R. Ewing of the TV soap opera *Dallas*. An example of the endless elasticity of children's folk traditions is a rhyme that popped up in Canadian school-yards in the early nineties at the height of Prime Minister Brian Mulroney's unpopularity. Based on the theme music from the popular *Tiny Toons* TV series, it went: "We're tiny, we're toony, we're all a little loony, 'cause Brian Mulroney invented GST."

Another way to shed light on the culture of childhood is to view it as a subculture, analogous to contemporary gay and lesbian subcultures. Just as children live in a world shaped by adults, gay men and lesbians live side by side with heterosexuals, sharing intimate bonds with them through family ties, friendships and work relationships. But over time gays and lesbians have developed their own separate realms, distinct subcultures set apart from the mainstream by shared sensibilities and tastes that straight people, as a rule, just don't get. Like Kid Culture, much of the focus of these subcultures is on play — on what gays and lesbians do to have fun. They may do much the same kinds of work as heterosexuals, but there may be real differences in the ways they choose to spend their leisure time. Not unlike children's culture, gay culture has for generations existed underground, devalued and ignored by the mainstream. The benefit of this, of course, is that gays and lesbians have been to some extent left to their own devices, to develop their collective identity without outside interference. The underground nature of these gay and lesbian subcultures also nurtured another trait they share with Kid Culture — a subversive sense of humour, a delight in mocking and actively undermining the powerful, oppressive majority.

But like any culture, childhood culture has its own distinctive character and traits: it is oriented to play and pleasure; it is subversive and anti-authoritarian; it favours the Image over the Word as its preferred mode of expression; and, despite two decades of feminism, it remains stubbornly sex-segregated.

KIDS JUST WANNA HAVE FUN

Play is the lifeblood of childhood. It's what children's culture is all about. Adults have somehow got the idea that "play" and "work" are antithetical, but for kids no such dichotomy exists. It is, quite simply, what they do, what they would spent all their time doing if they had the choice. Child development experts have studied the numerous functions that play serves in children's cognitive and social development. But in kids' own minds, play serves no "function" other than itself, other than living in the present, enjoying the moment. When Maria Montessori observed that "play is the child's work," she was stating an important truth, but one that is all too open to abuse. The tendency of adults, because of our distorted ideas about the value of play, our misguided abhorrence of "wasting time," is always to turn play into work, to impose an educational agenda on kids' play.

The play activities of babies and very young children involve a lot of what appears to be simple manipulation of materials — building with blocks, squeezing rubber balls and squeaky toys. But very early in life, usually between the ages of one and two, children begin to acquire the ability to pretend — to make objects "stand for" other objects, such as a spoon for a hammer, and to act "as if" they were an animal or another person. This is the beginning of imaginative play, a capacity that becomes more highly developed as children get older. We're all familiar with the marvellously elaborate play fantasies that four- and five-year-olds weave. They can go on for hours or end almost as soon as they begin, but they're always recognizable in one way or another as stories. From this age, the great bulk of kids' play activities involves pretending, making up stories, acting out fantasies. In large part, play consists of making narrative.

It's not just coincidence that the capacity for imaginative play and the beginnings of language development emerge in humans at the same time. There is a growing body of opinion that the ability to tell and think in "stories" forms the very foundation of human cognitive development. Speaking, reading, writing, even thinking itself are all activities that create narrative out of the chaotic jumble of mental activity and sensory experience. This storytelling activity doesn't involve only fictitious stories, but also "facts" — material and incidents from real life. The term "narrative" itself simply refers to a method of organizing facts, occurrences or imaginative material into some kind of shape and coherence, so that things "make sense."

Play is more than just making narrative — it's making narrative for no goal except pleasure. For fun. To paraphrase a mid-eighties pop song, "kids just wanna have fun." Adults don't quite know what to do with the fact that kids' thirst for play, for fun, is apparently boundless. It seems somehow indecent to us, this wanting to have nothing but fun, with no consequences, no price to pay. And we think of play as something that applies exclusively to childhood, especially to the pre-school and primary years. (Which doesn't mean adults don't play. We do, of course, but we prefer to use a more adult-sounding term like "leisure.") Play is so central to childhood that a severe lack of it will likely hinder a child's development in every area. And play and narrative are so intertwined that negative life experiences can have a profound impact on kids' imaginative capacities and their very ability to play. There is evidence, for example, that abuse and neglect can impair a child's ability to tell a story. In one study, a group of abused children had great difficulty when asked to relate an incident or tell a story from beginning to end. They became easily distracted, jumped around, did not seem to understand how the different elements were interrelated and, perhaps most tellingly, had difficulty connecting with the emotion of the story or incident.

In a very real sense, the world of play belongs to children. It's the one realm of experience they have every right to claim as their own. Child development experts like Jerome and Dorothy Singer, whose work is rooted in sympathetic observation of children in real-life play situations, acknowledge this. The Singers' 1990 book *The House of Make Believe: Play and the Developing Imagination* documents their many years studying children's play. They stress the fluid, organic, spontaneous nature of play and warn adults against interfering and trying to manage kids' play to fit their preconceived notions, however well-intended and "educational" they might be. But as much as enlightened experts like the Singers understand and appreciate the value of play, they don't necessarily view it the same way kids do. They believe play should be active: Kids making things, playing games, creating their own imaginative scenarios. But to kids' way of thinking, play is simply having fun — of any sort — and that includes playing hand-held video games or sitting and watching narratives created by others on a screen. This is the major function that pop culture serves for kids: as entertainment, as storytelling — a seemingly inexhaustible supply of stories. It's also what so disturbs adults: the thought that kids are spending so much of their time passively "consuming" all these stories.

But as so often where children are concerned, we adults seem to have a curious double standard around leisure activities.

Most of us spend a large part, perhaps the majority, of our non-working time in so-called passive activities — watching television, movies, plays, operas. But we find it somehow unseemly to allow children to do the same. "Watching" something just doesn't qualify as an activity, doesn't strike us as educational enough. Yet throughout history, humans have spent a large part of their leisure time being entertained — taking in stories thought up or told by others. Most cultures recognize that some people are better storytellers than others, and the community bestows the mantle of bard, *shanachie*, or *griot* on them. Most of the stories they told weren't particularly original, but retellings of tales already familiar to the listeners. It was accepted in traditional societies that both young and old would spend a good deal of their time in this way. Different as modern life is from these traditional ways, movies and television fulfil much the same function for those of us living in "wired" consumer societies. Drawing on common motifs, mythologies and familiar characters (especially in TV), they feed our own hunger for stories. They are, in a very real sense, the descendants of the old bards and storytellers. Also, in contrast to adults, who really do tend to be passive consumers, children are much more likely to put to use what they see, to transform it in their play and use it as a basis for their own imaginative creations.

THE DOMAIN OF PERSONAL POWER

Kid Culture is a culture of resistance and subversion, as adults fortunate enough to get a glimpse into kids' hidden world can discover. Their culture is the site of what little power and autonomy they have in the adult-controlled world, which Jerome and Dorothy Singer call the "Land of the Giants." Play, the Singers say, is children's "domain of personal power," and they identify a subversive quality that runs through much of kids' play. This subversive quality emerges as an impulse to "create a miniature social structure in which (children) can try out, under 'controlled conditions,' being 'bad' or disobedient." The Singers speculate that, in this way, play "serves an important balancing function for children in a world in which they are powerless."

Kids are smart enough to know they can't afford the luxury of open rebellion very often. They can't seize the means of production or the reins of power — how would they know what to do with them? But they are practical and adaptable. Like little guerillas, they seize power and free space wherever they can. And each generation discovers early on what oppressed peoples have always known: that there is exquisite satisfaction to be derived from making fun of their oppressors and imagining themselves in charge. Novelist and critic Alison Lurie explores this theme in her 1990 book *Don't Tell the Grown-Ups: Subversive Children's Literature*:

> Most of the great works of juvenile literature are subversive in one way or another .... They express ideas and emotions not generally approved or of even recognized at the time; they make fun of honored figures and piously held beliefs; and they view social pretenses with clear-eyed directness, remarking — as in Andersen's famous tale — that the emperor has no clothes.

For proof that children's culture is inherently anti-authoritarian, we have only to listen to some of the savage lyrics typical of time-honoured schoolyard rhymes:

> Row, row, row your boat gently down the stream
> Throw your teacher overboard, listen to her scream.

Anti-teacher songs like this and the one below are among the most popular and persistent of all the rhymes handed down through generations of schoolyard culture.

> On top of the schoolhouse, all covered with sand
> I shot my poor teacher with a red rubber band
> I shot her with glee, I shot her with pride
> How could I miss her? She was forty feet wide.
> I went to her funeral, I went to her grave

Some people threw flowers, but I threw grenades.
She looked up at me, she still wasn't dead
So I got a bazooka, and shot off her head.

In these songs, teachers are essentially stand-ins for the authority figures in kids' lives, especially the ones about whom they can't afford to express such fiercely negative sentiments — parents. Singing these songs, kids dare to speak the forbidden and imagine the unimaginable — that the power relations in their world could, for a time, be completely reversed.

These twin themes of speaking the forbidden and power relations are also among the most distinctive features of children's sense of humour, according to psychologist Martha Wolfenstein, who in the fifties wrote *Children's Humor*, likely the only study of the subject ever published. Though the classical Freudianism of her approach seems somewhat dated today, Wolfenstein's basic themes in *Children's Humor* still hold up. She shows how much of children's sense of humour is motivated by the drive "to transform painful and frustrating experiences and to extract pleasure from them." In children's case, the pain and frustration arise mostly from their relative powerlessness and the fact that they are not as free as adults to speak about what they know. Kids capitalize on the greater freedom allowed by jokes and silliness to rebel against this state of affairs — to speak the forbidden and reverse the existing power arrangements in their lives. This is the impulse, for instance, behind the long tradition of "moron" jokes of which kids are so fond. They derive great pleasure from conjuring up the image of a "stupid" adult, someone even stupider than they feel themselves to be. It's also the root of kids' bathroom humour, their fascination with sexuality and the bodily functions that are not to be spoken of in polite company. Added to this is very young children's sheer love of words and word play, especially "low" words like "pee-pee," with their repetitive, musical qualities and their outrageous connotations.

Modern pop culture has in many ways brought this subversive strain in Kid Culture more out in the open than ever. This is why kids are so attracted to it, and why adults — especially conservatively-minded adults — are so bothered by it. One of the pioneering influences in this hip, knowing, modern humour kids share is *Mad* magazine, still going strong after nearly four decades. When the magazine first appeared in the early fifties, psychologists and educators denounced it, along with comic books, for causing everything from juvenile delinquency to the spread of Communism. *Mad's* founder and publisher, William Gaines, was even called before U.S. Senate judiciary hearings on juvenile delinquency in 1954. I vividly remember the nuns at my own Catholic school forbidding us to read *Mad* and doling out heavy punishments when they happened to find a copy lurking at the bottom of a student's desk.

Though *Mad* was never aimed specifically at a school-age readership, it was discovered early on by teenagers who adopted it as their own. What the magazine did then, and continues to do now for an even younger readership, is introduce kids to the savage joys of parody and social satire. A large part of *Mad's* appeal, then as now, is its frank acknowledgement of the generation wars. Its editors understand only too well how much kids love the things their parents hate. A nearly lone voice in the fifties' ocean of conformity, *Mad* was willing to take on parents, politicians and other authority figures and gleefully expose their hypocrisy. It ought to be some consolation to contemporary parents that pop culture itself has become *Mad's* favourite target. Their send-ups of Teenage Mutant Ninja Turtles ("Teen Rage Moolah Nitwit Turtles") and the Simpsons (the "Simplesons") convey an admirably critical perspective on these TV mega-hits. In the world of *Mad,* nothing is allowed to become too big, too popular or too sacred to make fun of.

The Simpsons is itself the most recent heir to the *Mad* legacy of social satire and raising parental hackles. Many adults are upset by the negative role models the show supposedly fosters in Bart and Homer Simpson. But kids love what one boy called "the comedy of badness" that the show stands for. The Simpson kids are walking demonstrations of Wolfenstein's thesis that children turn their powerlessness into pleasure. The show's satirical edge lies precisely in the way it turns the happy-family/father-knows-best sitcom formula on its head. While managing to simultaneously draw on and send up the whole sitcom genre, the show also holds the mirror up to the bizarre role reversals that characterize so many contemporary, dysfunctional families: the parents, like Homer, are the children and the kids, like Lisa, have to be the grown-ups.

The work of popular Canadian children's author Robert Munsch also draws heavily on this subversive impulse. His books have been surprisingly controversial for a writer of good-natured picture books for pre-schoolers. But the frequent reversals of the adult-child power dynamic that runs through so many Munsch stories aren't lost on some hypersensitive adults. Munsch's book *Thomas's Snowsuit*, about a boy who refuses to wear an "ugly, brown snowsuit" in defiance of his mother, teacher and principal, has been banned by a number of Canadian school boards for "encouraging disrespect for authority." Another Munsch book that aroused even more controversy was *Giant, or Waiting for the Thursday Boat*, in which a giant threatens to "pound God into applesauce" for allowing Saint Patrick to drive all the snakes from Ireland. Some parents and educators were aghast to find a character in a Munsch book expressing anger, even threatening violence. But in his best work Munsch shows a keen understanding of kids' sense of humour and how their minds really work. The ritualized repetition of phrases in books like *Mortimer*, which can drive parents to utter distraction, is a source of real delight for pre-schoolers. Another Munsch book that caused a stir was *Good Families Don't* (more commonly known as "the fart book"), which mines kids' endless fascination with bodily functions and "speaking the forbidden."

I find Munsch's work interesting because it straddles the boundary between literature and popular culture. He writes books that elicit the kind of instant identification and exuberant responses we associate more with television. This may well be due to the fact that his stories are rooted in oral rather than literary traditions. Munsch got his start telling stories out loud to kids in the day-care centre where he worked, and even today he claims to develop his stories orally, trying out different versions many times before live audiences before committing them to paper. He also understands and uses with skill some of the ancient conventions of oral storytelling, such as having a character carry out an action three times, with variations each time, before advancing the story. But it is these very qualities of Munsch's stories (and more than a dose of literary snobbism) that lead children's book critics like Elizabeth MacCallum to dismiss them as "Miracle Whip" and "frenetic, quasi-hysterical versions of TV-on-paper."

WORD VS. IMAGE

The culture of childhood is even more profoundly subversive than the anti-authoritarianism found in *Mad*, *The Simpsons* and the books of Robert Munsch. What Alison Lurie calls children's "tribal culture" is forever finding ways to give expression to whatever is most feared or forbidden in the adult culture. Adults in modern industrial societies live (or like to think we do) in a world of facts, information, rationality. Meanwhile our children dwell alongside us in a land most of us have long left behind, a pagan culture where they keep alive many of the oral, iconic and mythic traditions of pre-industrial, pre-Christian societies.

One way to look at the culture gap between adults and

children is to see it as a tension between the Word and the Image — or, more mundanely, between "Read a book!" and "I want to watch TV." This tension was thoughtfully explored in a 1991 *Harper's* article featuring a debate on literacy and popular culture between Neil Postman and Camille Paglia. Postman is author of *Amusing Ourselves to Death* and other books that are sharply critical of the impact that popular culture and the new communications technologies have had on modern life and values. Paglia is an academic and popular culture enthusiast who gained considerable media notoriety (and the wrath of some feminists) in the early nineties for her pronouncements on Madonna and date rape. In her debate with Postman, Paglia argues that the modern pop culture phenomenon is a contemporary "eruption of paganism" from the underground into which it was driven by the rise of Christianity and scientific rationalism. The hunger for myth, for icons, which was once fulfilled by ritual and tribal traditions, is still strong in the modern world. According to Paglia, we turn to movies and rock stars to fill what is essentially a spiritual void.

Postman, playing the part of the worried parent, is deeply pessimistic about popular media's destructive effects on literacy and on children's capacity to sit still and think "in a realm that is unnaturally silent." He readily admits that promoting the importance of the Word to children is an uphill battle. "How," Postman asks, "can silence compete with television?" For her part, Paglia celebrates the very aspects of popular culture that most repel Postman. It is, she argues, bringing about the "repaganization of Western culture" and promotes a "multilayered, multitrack ability to deal with the world," a state of mind she says comes naturally to post-baby-boomers but that is quite foreign to those who, like Postman, came of age in the pre-television era. Interestingly, Paglia and Postman join forces when it comes to children's education, both concurring that it should be strongly "logocentric."

"The only defense against the seductions of imagery is a literate education," Postman insists. "If children are educated in the traditions of the word, then perhaps they will be able to make discriminating choices in the chaotic realm of the image."

The debate between Paglia and Postman not only gets to the heart of the Kid Culture dilemma, but also touches on many of the thorniest issues posed by the rise of computers and the five-hundred-channel universe. As I read their exchange of ideas, I kept thinking of the old Certs commercial in which a couple having a heated argument ("Certs is a candy mint!" "Certs is a breath mint!") is interrupted by the announcer breaking in and saying, "Stop! You're both right!" I am powerfully drawn to the energy and vitality of popular culture. But I was born in the late forties, I had a classical, liberal education and words are the very stuff of my work. I don't want to have to choose between the Image and the Word, and I don't want my children to have to, either. But I do think Paglia and other contemporary McLuhanites are right: the new electronic world order is a force that has to be reckoned with. The Image has to be honoured as an equally valid way of apprehending the world as the Word. But as in any major cultural upheaval, the transition can be difficult and anxiety-provoking. In the face of what looks like the Decline of Civilization as We Know It, it's no wonder that adults tend to seek refuge in a vision of a kinder, gentler childhood of yesteryear.

THE NOSTALGIA FACTOR

In April of 1992 the Toronto *Globe and Mail* carried a report about a school playground program in the Vancouver suburb of Coquitlam. Parents and teachers at Glen Elementary school, dismayed that their kids seemed to have so little knowledge of traditional children's activities like skipping rope and hopscotch, took on the task of teaching these skills themselves. One of them organized a group of parents to come to the playground twice a week, armed with skipping ropes, marbles and balls. According to the report, the adults' efforts were successful: They got the boys skipping rope, the too-cool older kids doing Double Dutch, and before long most of the kids were skipping and playing on their own, "without parental guidance." As the article noted, previous generations of kids had no need of parental intervention to learn these games and skills. They taught one another and passed them from generation to generation. The school's principal identified popular culture as the cause of the impoverishment of traditional children's culture: "They're heavily influenced by cartoons, Ninja Turtles and various other superheroes .... They're just modelling what they're seeing on television."

This principal's comment mirrors what has come to be the conventional adult wisdom about modern childhood: that it ain't what it used to be, that kids today are just products of the endless junk they watch on television. But I wonder if what we're seeing here is yet another example of the culture gap between adults and kids. It's impossible to tell from the article whether children's culture in Coquitlam really is "impoverished" or whether the adults were troubled because it didn't match their idea of what childhood should look like. By bringing in skipping ropes and marbles, the parents were clearly trying to enrich their children's lives by passing on activities they remember with pleasure. But they were also trying to recreate something recognizable in their terms, something that looked more like their own childhoods.

Nostalgia places an indelible stamp on adults' view of childhood. Typically, the adults of a given generation hark back to some former time for a picture of what they think childhood ought to be like. In our era, this ranges from the Victorian era in England to the small-town life of the forties and fifties. But whatever our point of reference, most adults find modern childhood — with its hip, knowing humour, its ubiquitous pop culture influences — foreign and threatening, not anything like what a "real" childhood should be. Bruno Bettelheim had a clear-eyed view of this nostalgia and how it influences adults' reactions to children and their culture. Towards the end of his life, he discussed how each generation of adults simultaneously deplores the newer forms of popular culture while retaining a soft spot for the older, familiar forms of their youth:

> Moralists, by nature, have always had a tendency to worry about and decry the newest dominant form of popular culture .... Any form of mass entertainment is viewed with considerable suspicion until it has been around for some time .... When I was a child, all kinds of evil influences were ascribed to the movies; today these are blamed on television. When I was a young man, the comics were denounced because they supposedly incited the innocents to violence .... New forms of entertainment are particularly suspect to adults who had no chance to enjoy them in childhood.

It's likely that the adult brain "reads" or takes in these entertainments in much the same way it did when we were children. So we enjoy them as we did then; we connect with them in a way we can't possibly connect with the newer forms that turn our kids on. Bettelheim's observations also underscore the irony of the axiom that yesterday's pop culture becomes today's classic, that "low" culture can acquire a patina of respectability over time and come to be considered art. Where Kid Culture is concerned this becomes doubly true, as the forms of play and entertainment of our youth become suffused with the golden glow of memory, of nostalgia for the happy childhoods we had (or wished we had).

So it's understandable that each generation of adults would try to recreate this rosy world of childhood for their own children. But this nostalgia leads to some ironic twists. Parents who wouldn't dream of buying their son a stuffed

Ninja Turtle, for instance, would be quite happy to see him fall asleep clutching a Teddy bear. But Teddy bears were the Ninja Turtles of their day, starting out as a popular craze at the turn of the century. They were named after U.S. President Teddy Roosevelt, whose reluctance to shoot a bear cub on a hunt led to a famous *Washington Post* cartoon of him with a bear cub on a leash. The Ninja Turtles may have a bad reputation for their tendency to fight at the drop of a hat. However, the original "Teddy"'s taste for violence (he once called war "the supreme triumph .... all the great masterful races have been fighting races") appears to have easily outstripped theirs. But that matters little today. The Teddy bear has come to be seen as a genteel toy with a vaguely Victorian pedigree reminiscent of more innocent times. But while we cling to this nostalgia-tinged view of childhood, the lives children actually lead are undergoing enormous upheaval, and their culture reflects those changes.

CROSS-GENERATION CULTURE

Not long ago my daughters and I watched an episode of *I Love Lucy*, a show that left an indelible stamp on my fifties' childhood. But I found there was no way I could communicate to them all the nostalgic associations I had. To them it was just another mildly amusing, curiously black and white TV show. But it's also true that the culture gap between me and my kids is considerably narrower than it was between me and my parents' generation. For all that I've stressed the separate and distinct world of childhood in this chapter, there are also vast areas of common culture between the generations. Rock music, which since its beginnings has belonged to adolescence, is now something kids can share with their parents. There are still generational differences, of course. Most adults my age hate rap music, for instance, and dismiss it as so much noise (much the same kind of thing our parents said about Elvis and the Rolling Stones, interestingly enough).

This intergenerational culture is a growing phenomenon in the entertainment industry, where shows like *The Simpsons* and Disney's *Aladdin*, which appeal equally to adults and kids, are becoming more and more the order of the day. "Family" films are more popular than ever, rivaling the action block-busters of the late eighties in their box-office grosses. And at the same time as traditionally children's genres like cartoons are appealing more and more to adult audiences, their content is also growing more sophisticated.

These are trends, but they may also be cultural signals that the historic trend identified by Philippe Ariès is reversing itself; the separate realms of adulthood and childhood, which became markedly distinct over the past several centuries, may be blending back into one another. The loss or shortening of childhood so lamented by social commentators like David Elkind and Neil Postman may actually be a swing of the pen-dulum, a return to the blurring of the boundaries between the adult and childhood realms that characterized the Middle Ages and that is still typical of many tribal societies today. As Ariès points out, these societies did not strictly separate chil-dren and adults either for work or play, nor did they share our modern preoccupation with shielding children from "adult" concerns like sex. Children would often be matter-of-factly exposed to entertainments whose bawdiness and profanity would make them unfit for children by our standards. But it is partly adults' own anxiety and ambivalence that give sex and profanity their powerful charge for kids. In my experi-ence, young children have only a passing interest in sex itself, but an abundant curiosity about anything they sense their parents don't want them to know about. Likewise, profanity holds such a keen fascination for children in part because adults' belief that these words are "bad" lends them an irre-sistible aura of power and danger. So even though we grudg-ingly accept the fact that kids nowadays have much more information about sex and more exposure to profanity, we still believe this violates the natural order of things. We say kids today are "growing up too fast," that childhood should be a time of innocence, of blissful ignorance of the seamier side of life. But clinging to a nostalgic view of childhood doesn't help us grapple with the reality that the culture of childhood, like any culture, has changed and continues to change.

CHAPTER THREE

Separate but Equal

THE SUCCESS OF the 1993 romantic comedy *Sleepless in Seattle* gave rise to a wave of media attention to the phenomenon of "chick flicks" and "guy pics." The film is structured around the Meg Ryan character's passion for the classic weepie *An Affair to Remember*, which in one key scene is contrasted with men's fondness for all-male war movies like *The Dirty Dozen*. These scenes openly acknowledge a fact that has long formed a backbone of the Hollywood film industry: Men and women like — and go to see — different kinds of movies. These differences in interests and taste between the sexes are so pervasive, and extend to so many areas of life, that we seldom find them worth commenting on. Women like to spend time shopping for clothes and watching soap operas. Men like to browse in hardware stores and watch sports on TV. Of course these are stereotypes that don't fit all men and women. But the thing about stereotypes is that they almost always contain a core of truth. The existence of distinct male and female cultures is a fact that adults of both sexes tend to accept with equal doses of bewilderment (for the other's tastes) and bemused tolerance. Yet any hint of extending this tolerance to the world of children tends to make modern, progressive-minded parents profoundly nervous. Those same differences in behaviour and taste that we accept with relative equanimity in ourselves set off alarm bells when we observe them in our kids. What we view as mere differences in adulthood we brand as sexist in childhood. But despite all our efforts to combat sexism, to encourage non-stereotyped play, to promote a unisex ideal, boys and girls continue to live in largely separate worlds through most of childhood. Kid Culture remains stubbornly sex-segregated, and, what's even more frustrating, much of the pressure to keep it that way comes from kids themselves.

Somewhere between the ages of three and four (not coincidentally, around the time imaginative play really comes into bloom), most children begin to show a preference for playmates of their own sex. They don't necessarily stop playing with kids of the opposite sex, but they do exhibit an awareness of group identity. They speak of "we" and "they," and are given to statements like "The boys at school play rough" and "Girls like pretty dresses." Many adults leap to the conclusion that these kinds of comments are purely the result of sexist conditioning they've already picked up from the larger culture. But I don't think that's necessarily all that's going on. When young children make their definitive-sounding pronouncements about "girls" and "boys," they may be mouthing propaganda about gender-appropriate behaviour. But they may also be engaged in a kind of thinking out loud, as they grapple with the huge new mystery of gender identity. If I am something called a girl, and he is something called a boy, what does this difference mean?

Adults have the luxury of having already figured out at least some of the mystery. We know that sex differences aren't everything, that males and females are alike in as many ways as they are different. The question doesn't loom as large for us, because we're more at home in the world. But for very young children, everything is large. Things take on mythic proportions. The story of life is new to them and they are struggling to understand it. Forging bonds with children of their own sex, forming a group identity as "girls" and "boys" may be one of the fundamental ways young kids get their bearings in a confusing world. Finally, at least one thing is relatively certain: I am a girl (or boy). I belong to the group, or tribe, of girls (or boys). I fit in somewhere in this chaotic scheme of things. This partly explains why kids seem to want clear distinctions between the sexes at this age, since this gives them at least the security of group identity and solidarity.

This marks the beginning of Girl Culture and Boy Culture. It now starts to become apparent to kids themselves that, for all they might have in common as people, girls and boys have different tastes, like to spend their time differently, even to some extent speak different languages. The world of young girls becomes intensely focused on relationships and maintaining beauty and harmony, a dynamic I'll be exploring in more detail later in this chapter. Boys, on the other hand, develop a passion for things, especially machines and vehicles of all kinds. What can possibly explain, for example, the run-away success among North American pre-school boys of *Road Construction Ahead*, a half-hour video consisting entirely of scenes of bulldozers, backhoes and rock crushers doing their work? This video had sold over 150,000 copies by late 1993, and there were reports of boys watching it hundreds of times over. To their mothers' eternal mystification, young boys also start to exhibit a fascination with grossness, an irresistible attraction to things ugly, hairy, slimy — the uglier, hairier and slimier the better. This explains at least part of the appeal of the Teenage Mutant Ninja Turtles, those slimy, cold-water amphibians, genetic mutants sired in ooze from a toxic sewer spill. One line of Ninja Turtles figures on the market had a sure-fire gimmick, from a boy's point of view: the figures secreted their own gross, greenish ooze! When a group of mothers fighting to get a Freddy Krueger (of *Nightmare on Elm Street* fame) doll off toy store shelves was interviewed on CBC Radio, it was clear that Freddy's appearance bothered them almost as much as his murderous behaviour. None of them could begin to fathom what their sons could possibly see in a creature so unspeakably ugly. What these mothers failed to take into account was that, for young boys, Freddy's very repulsiveness is his appeal. I've witnessed, and been just as mystified by it myself, a similar fascination with blood and guts in the boys' stories I've read over the years. Robert Bly makes the intriguing suggestion that, on a psychological level, this revelling in blood might be some kind of compensation for the fact that males lack "wounds," the bleeding and oozing that women's bodies do as a matter of course in menstruation and childbirth.

Modern parents become upset when the distinct cultures of boys and girls first make their appearance in the pre-school years. "Where do they learn it?" they say of sons obsessed with trucks and daughters obsessed with make-up. "Not from us!" This inevitably gives rise to the old nature/nurture debate: are these differences due to something in our genes, or is it all social conditioning? Feminists and others on the left end of the political spectrum have become understandably wary of biological explanations that view so-called inborn traits as carved in stone, fixed for all time. This kind of biological determinism was widely accepted as scientific doctrine in the nineteenth and early twentieth centuries and still has considerable currency among right-wing conservatives. But a similarly doctrinaire mind-set has taken hold among leftists and feminists, despite the existence of a credible body of scientific evidence for at least some inborn differences in male and female behaviour. In most progressive circles, it is now *de rigueur* to insist that all sex differences are "gender constructions" created by a sexist society with a stake in perpetuating, as one British feminist put it, a "false sense of mystery" between the sexes.

The reality, of course, is more complex than the extreme positions either camp takes. Though clearly some human behaviour is rooted in our genetic make-up, it's more accurate to say that nature gives rise to tendencies rather than traits, tendencies that are probably far more plastic and responsive to social stimuli than we imagine them to be. By the same token, if nature is more malleable than we think, I would also suggest that nurture or culture may not be so malleable or readily altered as we tend to assume. As I pointed out earlier, cultures are organic, multi-faceted entities that tend to have a mind of their own when confronted by humans with particular social or political agendas. To my mind, the concept of a rich, complex culture of childhood is far more helpful in understanding the behaviour of boys and girls than inherent biological differences. We don't spend a lot of time wondering, for instance, whether blacks developed musical forms like jazz, soul and blues because of something in their genes. We acknowledge that this music is part of their culture, a culture whose richness and integrity defy such one-dimensional, deterministic explanations.

For a vivid account of Boy Culture and Girl Culture in action, as well as its stubborn resistance to adult-engineered changes, we can look to the work of Chicago educator Vivian Gussin Paley. Over the past couple of decades, Paley has written a number of books based on her close observation of day-to-day life in her kindergarten classroom. She brings her pupils' world to life with great warmth and insight into their lives and into her own reactions and biases as well. Her 1984 book *Boys and Girls: Superheroes in the Doll Corner* is an absorbing account of the various imaginative dramas played out by the boys and girls in her class over the course of a year, and of her own — largely futile — efforts to re-direct their play in less sex-stereotyped directions. In one sense, the book is a remarkably clear illustration of the culture gap between children and adults. Paley herself is a gifted, sensitive teacher of many years' experience. But she readily acknowledges that despite her pupils' deep attachment to her, she is essentially an outsider in their world, a world whose workings still strike her as somewhat mysterious and unpredictable. Unlike most adults, Paley also has a deep-rooted respect for children's culture. At one point she tells the reader, "I have crossed an important threshold. Children's play has become more real to me than my own ideas of 'work'."

But the main focus of the book is on the kids themselves, or more specifically on what Paley terms "the five-year-old's passion for segregation by sex ... which no amount of adult subterfuge or propaganda deflects." In Paley's classroom, virtually every activity becomes an occasion for sex segregation, even forming a circle for storytime — girls on one side, boys on the other. She describes how, from the beginning of the year, the boys and girls marked out their respective territories in the classroom — the Doll Corner and the Building Blocks area — where day by day they proceeded to play out their often markedly different fantasy scenarios. The girls' clear preference was for "domestic play" — mother-and-baby scenes with periodic forays into more heightened fantasies involving princesses and mythical animal creatures. The boys concentrated on building and re-arranging block structures around which they could play out their superhero narratives, which at that point in time drew most of their inspiration from the popular *Star Wars* films.

The book documents the myriad ways in which boys' and girls' cultures are distinct from one another, distinctions that the kids themselves frequently comment upon. For example, a couple of boys inform Paley that "boys like bad smells .... We like stuff that isn't pretty, but not girls. They only like pretty things." Paley notes differences not only in the play scenarios, but even in the ways they are played out. The boys and girls in her class had quite different ways of dealing with the element of danger in play, for instance. The boys usually tried to master danger, typically by defeating a villain in battle. On the relatively rare occasions when the girls would conjure up a threat — perhaps a wild animal such as a lion — to intrude on their mostly serene domestic scenes, they would usually try to tame it, often having the intruder undergo a magical transformation into a "nice" non-threatening creature like a kitten. So, by quite different methods, both boys and girls would restore order and harmony to their play-worlds, however temporary. Like most North American kids, the children in Paley's class used popular culture as an inexhaustible source of material for their play narratives — *Star Wars*, various TV characters, Strawberry Shortcake and, of course, the ubiquitous Barbie. She also notes the ease with which they combine pop culture stories and figures with material from literary sources, traditional mythologies and fairy tales, brewing up an eclectic mixture peculiarly their own.

Paley's account of her own personal odyssey is every bit as absorbing as the dramas played out by the children, as she struggles with her ambivalence watching "the widening gap between boys and girls." At one point, somewhat against her instincts, she decides to intervene and see if, by encouraging the girls to do more building in the block area, she can bring about a less polarized play style in the classroom. The kids, not surprisingly, manage to thwart her efforts at every turn. To Paley's great credit, she understands that their drive to define themselves and control their own world is just as important as her desire to encourage non-stereotyped play, and she backs off. She also becomes increasingly aware of her own biases and their effects on the classroom dynamic. Paley acknowleged that, as a female herself, she finds it easier to relate to girls' play fantasies and Girl Culture in general. "When the children separate by sex, I, the teacher, am more often on the girls' side." Also, because boys' play tends to be more raucous and physical, they are continually coming into conflict with her teacherly desire for quiet, for a classroom that appears to an outsider to be "under control." By the end of the year, Paley has arrived at "an unavoidable conclusion: my curriculum has suited girls better than boys."

Quite a few modern parents will readily identify with Paley's ambivalence, since it mirrors our own. Many traditional cultures tend to be more matter-of-fact about the differences between the sexes than we are. They don't agonize over whether these are biologically determined or "social constructs" — they simply accept them as empirical realities. They are. This was a major theme of *Sex and Destiny*, Germaine Greer's provocative 1984 book that examined the lives of women in Third World tribal societies. Greer recognized that women in these traditional societies have their own particular cultural territories. She argues that although the differences in sex roles tend to be fairly rigidly enforced in these societies, this is not necessarily synonymous with Western-style sexism. On the contrary, Greer found that many of these societies accorded women great respect, and that their status within the society was rooted in this respect for women's traditional sphere.

Personally, I think the problem of sex roles lies less with the fact that boys and girls prefer separate realms than with the low esteem in which girls' culture is almost universally held. There is much fear and even loathing of boys' culture right now, the concern being that it glorifies war and violence. Boy Culture gets our dander up, but at least we accord it power and a certain amount of respect. But while Boy Culture is demonized, Girl Culture continues to be trivialized. The things that girls and women naturally gravitate to — Barbie and pretty clothes, soap operas and romance novels — are routinely dismissed as silly activities fit only for mindless idiots. Feminists can sometimes be the worst offenders in this regard. We are understandably wary of how "feminine" preoccupations have been used to trivialize us for so long. But in our zeal to break free of the constraints of imposed sex roles, we also run the risk of passing on to our daughters those same demeaning, dismissive attitudes towards female culture itself. While the things that males do and like have status by definition, the things that females do and like do not — a double standard that is still largely accepted by men and women alike.

This devaluing of female culture is so pervasive we seldom recognize it for what it is. We wring our hands over the fact that so few girls are attracted to traditionally male fields like math and science, for example, but we rarely bemoan the under-representation of boys in dance classes and school choirs. We cry out for more women in politics, but rarely for more men to be day-care workers (we know they'd never stand for the crummy pay). Boys' sports-card trading is a multi-million-dollar industry, while stickers, girls' favourite trading commodities, occupy the turnaround racks in low-end stores like Zeller's. Mark Twain's *Huckleberry Finn* is considered a literary classic, while Lucy Maud Montgomery's *Anne of Green Gables,* for all its enduring popularity, has never been accorded respect as a work of serious literature. And the list goes on. While it's vital for girls to have examples like astronaut Roberta Bondar to inspire them to an unlimited range of possibilities, it's important to remember that these kinds of role models don't convey any particular value for more typically female experience. And given the lack of respect accorded the female sphere in our culture, it's not at all surprising that young boys are so eager to distance themselves from it. Maybe what we need is not a unisex culture for children, but ways to engender greater respect for female culture.

AT PLAY IN THE ALL-FEMALE UNIVERSE

One consequence of the recent flurry of concern about rising levels of violence is that the culture of boyhood has come under intense scrutiny. With their passion for war toys and their more aggressive play styles, boys are regarded as the Big Problem of the moment. Which also means that, as usual, they get most of the attention. Meanwhile, the "good" girls go about their business quietly, almost in secret. The lives of girls and women, to borrow Alice Munro's title, go on as they always have — overlooked, unsung, undervalued. When it does attract adult notice, Girl Culture, like Kid Culture in general, is more often than not misunderstood. To most adults, including (perhaps especially) feminists, it looks like little more than a bundle of stereotyped notions and behaviours, the sum total of patriarchal conditioning from birth.

But also like Kid Culture, girlhood culture is in many ways a culture of resistance. What looks to us like sex-role stereotyping is often the result of young girls' insistence on putting female experience at the centre rather than on the periphery of life, their resolute upholding of female interests and traditions in a world that gives them little value or importance. In many ways, feminism in its purest form is found in four- and five-year-old girls. There is absolutely no doubt in their minds about the value of being a girl and of female experience. For them, the entire universe revolves around femaleness — mothers and princesses, Barbies and unicorns. In a sense, they live in an Eden where Woman has not yet fallen from grace, where She is not yet considered peripheral, second-class, Object rather than Subject.

Certain themes emerge in these early years that characterize girls' lives through girlhood and beyond. Harvard psychologist Carol Gilligan has begun to map this hidden terrain of girls' culture in her work on female psychological development. In her 1982 book *In a Different Voice*, Gilligan described how girls make moral choices based on an "ethic of care," in which their main priority is to maintain interpersonal bonds and avoid hurting others. Girls' ethical decision making, Gilligan found in her study, differed significantly from boys' (and from what most developmental theorists regard as "normal") in that they focused more on feelings and relationships and less on abstract notions of right and wrong. Her latest book, *Meeting at the Crossroads: Women's Psychology and Girls' Development,* co-written with Lyn Mikel Brown, continues this exploration of the girls' inner lives through an intensive, five-year series of interviews with girls on the cusp of adolescence. Their work confirms that, up until pre-adolescence, it is the bonds between females that are all-important, that girls' social lives revolve largely around one another. Their interviews reveal young girls' over-riding concern with interpersonal relationships and their constant efforts to maintain connectedness and harmony in those relationships. This concern with bonds and togetherness is reflected in the very language that girls use: *Meeting at the Crossroads* cites studies showing that they tend towards a more "collaborative" style of speech than boys, who prefer a more "controlling" speaking style.

This overwhelming emphasis on relationships can certainly have its down side. As parents of daughters can attest, girls' friendships can be a constant round of fever-pitch emotions, petty resentments and dramas of exclusion. Their efforts to avoid conflict can clearly work against them, when they swallow their own anger and put aside their own needs to avoid hurting someone else. This desire to avoid hurt can have lifelong consequences, too. Biologist Karen Messing told a 1993 conference on gender and science that routine laboratory procedures like dissecting frogs are part of what keeps women out of these fields: "A surprising number of girls are just put off by having to do mean things to animals."

Right from the time it becomes "pretend" play and begins to take on a narrative shape, girls' play reflects this emphasis on relationships. In their play little girls create an essentially all-female universe, a golden world bathed in a glow of love and harmony, with not a metaphorical hair out of place. Of course, this world is just that: a metaphor, an imaginative creation, an ideal to be aspired to rather than lived in. In everyday life little girls can be just as messy, anarchic and irreverent as the rest of us. But this aesthetic of beauty and harmony pervades girls' play-worlds. It gives rise to their passion for "prettiness," for colours like pink and purple, for decorating their bodies with lipstick and nail polish. Adults routinely disparage this love of adornment, in the belief that it all stems from sexist conditioning. But there's also a delicious sensuality in this girlish pursuit of beauty, and some of their moments of deepest bonding occur at these times. In *Boys and Girls*, Vivian Paley describes the "hushed excitement," the almost ritualized air of mystery that pervades her kindergarten class when the girls gather to apply nail polish to one another's hands.

Toy manufacturers, of course, have this young female aesthetic down pat. They know all the right buttons to push, because they understand just how deeply little girls want to believe that they really are made of sugar and spice and everything nice, that love really does rule the world. Season after season toy makers carry these themes to saccharinized extremes, turning out infinite variations on collectibles like My Little Pony, gimmick dolls like Little Miss Magic Jewels, and, of course, baby dolls whose capacity for love and nurturing knows no bounds. Unlike boys' collectibles like Micromachines and Transformers, which emphasize conflict and high-tech weaponry, girls' universes reflect the eternal struggle to maintain harmony and beauty in the face of strife and ugliness. Rainbow Brite, a popular collectible and animated feature subject from the mid-eighties, is a good example of this theme. Rainbow and her cohorts, the Color Kids, have an over-riding mission: keeping the world safe for colour and beauty. They are locked in a never-ending battle with the evil Murky Dismal and his pea-brained sidekick Lurky, whose counter-mission is to drain colour from the world, making it grey and lifeless. In contrast to the larger society, these play-worlds are overwhelmingly female-dominated. There are no males to be seen in My Little Ponyland, for example, whose pastel-maned inhabitants with names like Moondreamer and

Bluebell are all unmistakably female. The Rainbow Brite universe has a few token boys like Red Butler and Buddy Blue, as well as the villainous male interlopers Murky and Lurky. But in girls' play-worlds, it is mostly females who drive the stories and set the tone.

Dolls are another central and enduring fact of girls' culture. Feminists aren't entirely comfortable with the whole idea of dolls. We tend to see them as more gender conditioning for the traditional role of wife-and-mother, and we'd be just as happy, if not happier, to see our daughters outside riding bikes and building forts. Boys and dolls are another matter. Many progressive parents swear they'd be thrilled to see their sons playing with dolls. But the reality is that dolls are a "girl thing" in our culture, which gives them an automatic stigma. Despite decades of feminism, boys' resistance to dolls is as strong as it ever was, and many adults quietly share their disdain.

Doll play is certainly quieter, and seemingly more passive, than the rough-and-tumble of typical boys' play. As Dorothy and Jerome Singer point out in *The House of Make-Believe*, girls' play in general is "more symbolic and covert" than boys', but they believe it's anything but passive. Though much of doll-play is quiet and involves sitting relatively still, there is a wealth of internal, imaginative "action" going on. One adult who has explored the intense, complex relationships girls have with their dolls is British novelist Rumer Godden. Her children's stories frequently feature dolls as actual characters, dolls who are often expressions of their girl-owners' souls, their inner spirits. Like real live girls, Godden's doll characters have an all-encompassing need for connection and "come alive" only when touched and played with. And like human girls, the dolls in her books are afflicted with powerlessness and a literal lack of voice: They must wait to be chosen by their human owners and can communicate with them only through the intuitive, almost telepathic vehicle of wishing. The climactic moments in many of Godden's doll stories occur when the doll's wishes and longings are finally "heard" by her human owner, or when girl and doll are finally united as soul mates, as in *The Story of Holly and Ivy*. But Godden is no sentimentalist, and her stories also unflinchingly portray the cruelty young girls often inflict on their dolls and one another. Nor are her doll characters passively resigned to their fate; they constantly resist their powerlessness. In *Impunity Jane*, for example, a tiny but strongly made doll ("You could drop her with impunity") belongs to a series of girls who keep her confined to a doll-house. Impunity Jane longs to escape and find adventure in the outside world. Finally a boy named Gideon braves the taunts of his playmates and adopts her. He carries her around in his pocket, and as he rides his bike, Impunity Jane peers out and watches, with an exhilarating sense of freedom, the wide world whizzing by.

THE BARBIE CONUNDRUM

Doll fashions have come and gone over the years, but for many girls, there is only one Doll, and her name is Barbie. There may be nothing more vexing for modern, liberated parents than a daughter's inevitable craving for a Barbie. Yet no toy is more misunderstood by adults than Barbie. Certainly she is a singular phenomenon in the toy world, accounting for sales of nearly $1 billion annually for her manufacturer, Mattel. Having weathered decades of changing toy fashions and feminist wrath, Barbie has become far more than a mere consumer item. She has become a totem, an icon. She has entered the realm of mythology.

To adults, Barbie's only mission in life appears to be to look beautiful, go to parties and shop till she drops. But this impeccably turned-out Barbie is largely a creature of Mattel's marketing department and doesn't bear much resemblance to girls' real-life play. Those tiny spike heels of hers invariably go missing within hours of purchase, and her gauzy ball gowns become pretty tatty before long. Before you know it, Barbie's having a permanent bad hair day and spending most of her time without a stitch on. The truth is that girls are constantly subverting the script laid out in the Barbie ads. However much Mattel may intend Barbie to be a paean to consumerism and traditional notions of femininity, it's been my observation that little girls remake her in their own image and use her as a celebration of their own femaleness. In their play fantasies, Barbie doesn't just sit around looking pretty. She's just as likely to pile into her hot pink Corvette with a gang of other Barbies and Ariel the Mermaid (Barbie owners never discriminate against dolls made by other manufacturers) and head off looking for adventure.

In actual fact, Barbie is a very adaptable, open-ended toy. Over the past few years the doll market has become increasingly geared to expensive, high-concept dolls that "do" something, like Baby RollerBlade, Baby All Gone (who "eats" cherries from a spoon) and Magic Potty Baby (guess what she does). Child development experts tend to be critical of these toys because they limit spontaneity: the toy directs how the child will play with it. Mattel has itself made periodic forays into this arena with Barbie. In 1992 the company brought out a talking version, Teen Talk Barbie. But after the novelty wore off (and, as so quickly happens with these "activity" toys, the talking function broke down), girls found they were just as happy to go on doing Barbie's talking for her — and Lord knows they do a more interesting job of it than Mattel.

Barbie is not only a low-concept toy, she's also a quintessential example of what media analyst John Fiske calls an open or "producerly" text, which can be "read" or experienced in a variety of ways unintended by her creators. One woman told me she overheard her daughter and a friend one day decide that their Barbies would be lesbians and fall in love with one another. Earring Magic Ken, whom Mattel brought out as part of an Earring Magic Barbie line in 1993, has become an instant icon and in-joke for gay men, despite the company's insistence that he's just a fun, wholesome toy for young girls. And Ken himself is far from being the centre of Barbie's universe. Doting grandparents may purchase Ken dolls, but that doesn't mean little girls are actually going to play with them. When they deign to do so, Ken is consigned to playing the boyfriend, the kind of supporting role that women have always played in male-centred stories. Writer Marnie Jackson comments that Ken looks like nothing so much as a "rented gigolo, or the guy who takes Barbie's outfits to the cleaners and back." Girls have no real need of Ken, because with Barbie, we are still in the all-female universe, where the bonds between females — between Barbies, between girls — are what's important. Another way in which Barbie is misunderstood lies in her preoccupation with adornment. Girls are quite definite that the major appeal of Barbie lies in dressing her up in "pretty things." But if you ask them if all this adornment is for the benefit of Ken and other males, you draw a complete blank. There's no doubt in their minds that all the prettiness, the endless dressing-up and changing of outfits, is for their own pleasure.

Much of the misunderstanding arises from the fact that most adults have long forgotten their own childhood play experiences and have only a dim understanding of the complexity of fantasy play. They assume that toys like Barbie have a single, clear message that is swallowed whole. Kids themselves have a much better intuitive grasp of the multi-faceted relationship between reality and fantasy. Girls know that Barbie is a fairy princess, a goddess. She belongs in the realm of the ideal, of archetype. They often articulate this view to adults when given the chance. From time to time I've asked young girls if they want to look like Barbie, if playing with Barbie makes them feel they ought to look like her. They usually look at me like I've just landed from Mars. One 11-year-old of my acquaintance, who is considered a rabid feminist in her circle, told me that, although she used to love playing with Barbies, she now had to admit they were "a little bit sexist." Did she think, then, that girls shouldn't be allowed to play with Barbies at all? My friend looked stunned at the suggestion. That, she replied with utmost firmness, would be going too far.

This isn't to suggest that Barbie and other dolls are harmless and have no impact outside of some rarefied fantasy realm. My own gripe with Barbie has to do with her contribution to our culture's tyranny of thinness (in which, of course, she's far from being the sole offender). Barbie could still be beautiful without having such a distorted body shape. There's nothing to prevent Mattel, in line with their long-standing practice of providing "alternative" Barbies with black hair, darker skin or Asian features, from bringing a fuller-bodied Barbie onto the market. A "Big, Bold and Beautiful Barbie" could have an impact on girls' concerns about body image that would far outstrip adult reassurances that "you don't have to be thin to be beautiful." But, as Marnie Jackson observes, it's Barbie's very "lack of redeeming social value," her refusal to be "educational" that have played a large part in her enduring popularity. She continues to take the better part of her cues from her girl-owners rather than from their parents or her own maker, Mattel.

Adult opposition to Barbie dies hard, however. Controversy erupted in the fall of 1992, when Mattel brought the aforementioned Teen Talk Barbie onto the market. One of the phrases in her repertoire, "Math class is tough," prompted an outcry from feminists, who complained that it perpetuated the stereotype that girls are no good at math. Despite the fact that the voice chips in Teen Talk Barbies contained a huge number of possible phrases (one company official estimated the chances of getting one with the math class phrase at one in four thousand), Mattel launched its first product recall in 33 years of Barbie history. Reassuring the public that it had no intention of fostering sexist stereotypes — after all, another Teen Talk Barbie phrase was "I'm studying to be a doctor" — Mattel offered to replace any Teen Talk Barbie saying the offending phrase. Interestingly, Mattel's announcement was met with a resounding silence, prompting what may have been the smallest consumer response to a product recall in corporate history. Shortly before Christmas of 1992, the company announced that out of many thousands sold, a grand total of five Teen Talk Barbies had been returned in the United States and Canada. The reason? Mattel's announcement had made the doll an instant collector's item, increasing its value by several hundred dollars almost overnight. To add to the irony, overall sales of the doll shot up as consumers rushed to buy it in hopes of scoring one with the "math class" phrase. Once again Barbie showed her incredible resilience and adaptability, as Mattel executives watched the controversy turn into a bonanza of free publicity.

But there does appear to be at least the beginnings of a feminist "re-visioning" (to borrow a term from modern deconstructionism) of Barbie on the horizon. In the spring of 1992, the alternative-press digest *Utne Reader* carried an article in which a number of women writers and artists praised Barbie as a "revolutionary" and a "feminist trailblazer." Barbie is also increasingly turning up as a kind of deconstructed text in feminist art. Popular performance artist Meryn Cadell included a piece on Barbie on her first album, for example, and Toronto artist April Hickox has used Barbie outfits in a series of photographic studies of women's lives. From sex goddess to feminist nemesis to postmodern *objet d'art:* you sure have come a long way, Barbie.

When Girls Tell Stories

If play is about making narrative, doll play is about making female narratives. When they play with dolls, girls are weaving fantasies in which female experience is at the centre of the story, in which the leading roles (usually all the roles, in fact) are female. Doll play marks the earliest outward stage of girls' absorption in female-centred stories, an absorption that preoccupies most girls right through the pre-school and primary years. I've observed another early indicator of this preoccupation in the strong preference girls seem to have for drawing pictures of females. Most kids begin to draw recognizably human figures around age four, and from the start little girls' drawings are typically of females. As their co-ordination and fine motor skills develop, they render more and more detailed and vivid depictions of the most distinctive female features: hair, eyes, lips. Though the world around them treats male experience as the norm, little girls' drawings indicate that their inner world is still largely a female-centred one.

When girls start telling stories verbally and acting them out, the "golden world" of female culture, with its themes of love, harmony and beauty, emerges strongly there, too. Vivian Paley noted that in the Doll Corner of her kindergarten class, the action of the girls' play fantasies typically centred on a cast of mothers and babies — human or animal — with intermittent appearances by such fairy tale characters as princesses, fairy godmothers and unicorns. This largely female world carries over into their early efforts at writing stories as well. I've seen this familiar array of stories about friendship between appealing — and mostly female — animal characters again and again in the stories I've read by seven- and eight-year-old girls. But soon after this, around age nine or so, girls' narratives start to undergo a shift, which becomes more and more prominent as they approach adolescence. This near-exclusive focus on female concerns and female characters that marks the primary years begins to fade. As we'll see in the next chapter, the society around them finally begins to make serious inroads into girls' culture, as they discover that in the larger world, it's the male, not the female, who is at the centre of the story.

CHAPTER FOUR

The Case of the Missing Hero(ine)

IN THE EARLY CHILDHOOD YEARS, boys and girls show a marked preference for members of their own sex, both as playmates and as the subject matter of their play-fantasies. But this preference is somewhat less pronounced in girls. As Vivian Paley noted in her kindergarten classroom, the boys "scrupulously disregard female characters" in their play and stories. As one of the girls complained to her, "The boys never put girls in their stories. Then they get all the turns when it's their stories to act." The girls in her class, on the other hand, occasionally include male characters and "try out ideas with a male stamp." A similar dynamic is noted by Jerome and Dorothy Singer in their exploration of the "imaginary friend" phenomenon so prevalent in childhood. Girls, they point out, frequently create imaginary friends who are male, while boys never create female imaginary friends.

This difference becomes even more marked as children move into middle childhood. When I began doing story-writing workshops in the schools, I immediately noticed what amounted to an unwritten law: boys write stories about males, while girls write stories about both sexes. In the boys' universe, females essentially did not exist. The protagonists in boys' stories were always, without exception, male, and all the important relationships were between males. Even the violence was done by males to other males. The boys' stories I read were, in essence, extreme examples of the "buddy" genre we see so often in Hollywood movies. If a female character managed to make her way into the story, she almost never figured significantly in the action, but served instead as a plot device — usually a princess who spends the duration of the story in some off-stage castle waiting to be rescued. As an experiment I once asked a couple of boys I knew quite well if they would try writing stories with a main character who was female. I was curious to see what they would come up with, and at first they seemed quite agreeable to the idea. Then several weeks of stalling ensued, and when the stories failed to materialize, it dawned on me that my request may have been a lot harder for them to fulfil than I realized at first. Much as I knew they liked and respected me, they just couldn't bring themselves to do it, because I was in reality asking them to break an important "boy" taboo.

The universe of the girls' stories, on the other hand, was a much more mixed one. Though they often wrote about female characters, they were just as likely to build a story around a male protagonist as a female one. The stories by these eight-, nine- and ten-year-old girls clearly showed they were beginning to venture beyond the cute-animal phase, the blissful domestic realm of their early childhood play, and starting to explore other stories and genres — mysteries, sci-fi, adventure. But this broadening of their interests also coincided with a more pronounced male presence in their stories. In fact, the more active the protagonist and the more action-oriented the story, the more likely the girl-author was to choose a male as the main character.

None of this is the least bit surprising, of course. It's no wonder boys make no space for females in their stories, when they so rarely see a female depicted as the central character of any story. It's no wonder girls need to create male protagonists when they start wanting to experience adventure in their stories. Who else is there to identify with but males? Both girls and boys are simply following the existing storytelling models they're already familiar with, from literature and high art as well as from television and movies. This overwhelming dearth of female-centred stories makes both girls and boys reluctant to value and identify with female experience. Reading kids' stories over the past few years has convinced me that this lack of stories about girls and women is a more deep-rooted problem in popular culture than violence or stereotypes. Everywhere children look only one side of the equation is being represented. By and large, only one story is being told: the male quest tale.

Given this overwhelming male-centredness in our existing storytelling models, it's heartening and somewhat remarkable that girls persist in putting themselves and their experience at the centre of their stories as much as they do. In doing so they're swimming against a current that reaches back centuries, if not millenia. Joseph Campbell, whose writings on mythology have become popular over the past couple of decades, explores the dimensions of the hero-quest story in various mythological traditions in his book *The Hero with a Thousand Faces*. These quest tales, or "monomyths" as Campbell calls them, have some striking cross-cultural similarities, chief among them the fact that the hero is universally male. Females, when they appear in the quest tale, are defined in relation to the hero — as wife, as mother, as the "prize" to be won or rescued. A look at Campbell's index gives a good sense of the role women characters play in the hero's story: "Woman: symbolism in hero's adventure, as goddess, as temptress, as hero's prize; see also mother." Nowhere in the book does Campbell himself consider the possibility that "woman" could serve the same function as the hero, that she could in fact be the hero, the one whose actions drive the story. Admittedly, the epic or quest tale tradition supports him in this. Though there are quite a few creation myths from various cultures that feature female deities, there are no surviving epics in world literature that centre on a female hero. (The folk and fairy tale traditions give a quite different picture where women are concerned, which I'll be exploring in the next chapter.)

We have trouble even conceiving of a female "hero"; there are no models to draw on. Even the language stands in our way. "Hero" is by definition male. The *Oxford English Dictionary* defines it as the "chief male personage in a poem, play or story." The female counterpart, "heroine," simply doesn't carry the same weight. Though Oxford defines it as "the principal female character in a poem, story or play," we don't necessarily think of a heroine as the focus of a given story. She might simply be the hero's love interest. Phrases like "our heroine" have a distinct whiff of condescension similar to terms like "poetess" that have justifiably fallen into disrepute.

What these terms do is simply reflect the reality of woman's true position in narrative: she is, to use Simone de Beauvoir's term, the Other. She is not the subject, the centre, the focus, not even of her own life. As linguist Deborah Tannen argues, to be female is to be "marked" as other-than-primary. So a female character has no independent existence, but rather serves a function — though possibly a very key one — in the hero's story. Of course this is true, to varying extents, of all the "supporting" characters, male or female, in a given story. They all exist to serve some function or reflect some quality for the hero or protagonist. But males are accustomed to seeing one of their own as the central figure in a narrative. The problem for women, the problem that surfaced again and again in the stories by young girls I read, is that we are still "marked," still largely confined to "other" status. We still have so little opportunity to see "our kind" at the centre of the stories we see and hear. Even the modern "anti-hero" is never a woman. He's too much of an Everyman, bespeaking a kind of universality from which females are excluded.

Two decades of the modern feminist movement have begun, but only begun, to make a dent in this situation. Stories with a female protagonist, recounting female experience, told from a female point of view, are still few and far between. And for this, popular culture is no more nor less to blame than "high" culture. As I'll try to show in the next chapter, contemporary popular culture is the site of some very interesting developments in female-centred narrative. But first, the bad news.

THE OTHER WOMAN

One day in September 1992 I was reading the arts section of my local daily paper. The Toronto Film Festival was in progress, and I perused accounts of half a dozen festival films that explored the theme of childhood in some way. All the films featured male protagonists. The female journey through childhood, at least in that year's crop of films, was absent. I turned to a long piece on how Canadian animation studios are becoming major players in the international sphere. The story featured no fewer than ten animated features or TV specials currently in development (as they say in the industry). Eight of these had male protagonists. One had a male/female team as its central characters. The last, the only one written by a woman, was focused on a group of characters — a family.

A not unusual day. The dearth of female-oriented narratives is an old story. What is new, and somewhat heartening, is the fact that it's at least beginning to be noticed; it's no longer considered so normal as to be invisible. Major Hollywood actresses like Sissy Spacek and Barbra Streisand are now regularly quoted decrying the lack of good female roles in feature films. A 1993 *Maclean's* cover story devoted to women in Hollywood revealed, among other things, that the Oscar-winning *Howard's End* was originally rejected by a male studio executive as "too soft, too sensitive." The stature of male actors becomes enhanced as they grow older, but women find there's no place for them in feature films once they're "too old" to play the love interest, a problem not faced by male actors. Michelle Pfeiffer comments in the same *Maclean's* piece, "I'm very aware that this is my window of time" and points out that she played opposite 60-year-old Sean Connery in *The Russia House* "and nobody batted an eye." And that window of time may be even narrower than it's generally thought to be. For while family films starring child actors like Macaulay Culkin are more popular than ever, the vast majority of the stories centre on boy characters. As 13-year-old Christina Ricci, star of *Addams Family Values*, told a reporter in late 1993, "Everyone talks about women getting snubbed but what about little girls? We have no parts either. It's all for little boys. And if it's a little girl's part, it's minuscule. It's the girlfriend waving 'hi' and that's it." The harsh reality is that in Hollywood, the box office rules, and films featuring girls simply don't have the same financial clout. Culkin's two *Home Alone* movies were monster hits, while *Monkey Trouble*, an appealing comedy about a girl and her larcenous pet monkey that bore some similarity to the *Home Alone* formula, did only modest business in its theatrical release.

Television comes considerably closer to reflecting female reality: nearly half of all TV characters in 1990 were female, compared to less than a third in feature films. This isn't so surprising, given that television tends to deal more with real-life problems like family violence, in contrast to the more mythic, larger-than-life "hero" stories that seem so at home on the big screen. But consequently many of these roles for fortysomething actresses, even when they are the lead, are "victim" characters. For every Murphy Brown and Roseanne Arnold, there's a battered wife, a rape victim, a brave mother battling the disease-of-the-week.

The picture looks no better when we turn our attention to

children's television. With the odd exception such as Disney's *Little Mermaid,* female main characters and female-oriented stories were until recently almost non-existent in the kid-dominated Saturday morning domain. Periodic attempts to bring on female-centred cartoons like Nelvana's *Little Rosey* (about a character based on Roseanne Arnold's childhood) promptly bit the dust. In fact, in the early eighties, there were more girl-oriented cartoon shows such as *My Little Pony* and the superhero *She-Ra,* than there were at the beginning of the nineties. People in the industry contend the situation is dictated by the bottom line rather than sexism. Advertising revenues are based on audience size and, in the words of one industry executive, "You have to have boys watching a show for it to succeed .... It is well known that boys will watch a male lead and not a female lead. But girls are willing to watch a male lead." This, of course, is the same dynamic we saw at work in kids' stories: girls are apparently quite comfortable identifying with male heroes and male experience, while boys appear to be profoundly uncomfortable, and highly resistant to, identifying themselves with anything even remotely female. And, as another industry executive points out, "When there are a boy and a girl in the room, it would appear that the boy controls the TV set." This, in a nutshell, is the major obstacle to female-centred narrative: the perception that it's somehow not of general interest. That is, while we regard the male-hero story as the norm and expect girls and women to spend lifetimes watching stories built around male protagonists, we simply don't expect the same of boys and men. Female experience is still considered a specialty, a side dish.

I'm not suggesting that it's somehow unnatural for women to identify with male experience, or vice versa. Not everything has to be gender-determined. I certainly don't restrict my interests to "female" subjects. I love Westerns, for example, about as "male" a genre as they come. But the problem resides in the enormous narrative imbalance. Stories have the power to shape our view of reality. If girls rarely see stories that reflect their own experience, how can they learn to value it themselves? If women rarely see stories that put female characters at the centre, how do we learn to see ourselves at the centre of our own story, of our lives?

Everywhere we look, both in children's literature and popular culture, we see a vacuum. Representation of one-half of the human race is largely missing. It extends to things as innocuous as those adorable but almost universally male animal creatures that populate so much of the children's landscape. One charming children's classic, *Play with Me*, has, admirably, a female main character, a young girl who approaches various forest animals to play with her. But from the book you wouldn't know that females even existed in the animal kingdom: the creatures are all male. For years when I read this book to my daughters, I routinely changed half the "he's" to "she's" for the animals. But I was always aware of the extra effort it took to do this, and my kids could tell that I wasn't reading exactly what was on the page. Though it has long been considered a model of social equity in every other way, *Sesame Street* was on the air almost 25 years before it achieved anything approaching gender balance in the Muppet population. It seems so little to ask that a realistic proportion of these characters be female, but it's rarely the case. *The Illustrated Encyclopedia of Cartoon Animals* illustrates just how large this void of female depiction is. An exhaustive compendium that spans animation's earliest days to the present, the book lists over two thousand animal cartoon characters and less than 10 percent of these are female. What few girl characters there are in cartoons usually have some obviously "feminine" characteristics — they're cats, for example, or someone's mother. They are routinely denied the variety and range of attributes that male characters enjoy as a matter of course.

The "otherness" of female experience pervades most of the popular storytelling genres. The boys in a coming-of-age movie like *Stand by Me* learn about the Big Themes of life and death. Together they experience an adventure that brings them to a kind of maturity; they come into their power. But girls' coming-of-age stories almost always involve learning about love and relationships, a sexual coming-of-age more than anything else. Even a fairly with-it, contemporary film like the hit *My Girl*, about an 11-year-old aspiring poet who has to confront the death of her best friend, undercuts itself with its title. It's the girl who is the subject of the film, but "*My Girl*" suggests that she's the object of someone else's gaze.

Enormous, wide swaths of female experience are simply missing from popular narratives. Females are rarely shown in relationship to one another, for example. Male bonds, the "buddy" movie, the son searching for reconciliation with the father — these are the narrative themes that appear again and again in pop culture and literary genres. When women appear in these stories at all, they are typically depicted in near-total isolation from each other, with all their emotional energy focused on a son, husband or lover. Or, if they're "liberated," they usually can't be bothered with other women. They'd rather hang out with the boys, like April O'Neill on *Teenage Mutant Ninja Turtles*. And though the mother bond is sentimentalized and mythologized as the source of all love and caring, mothers as characters, as real people with recognizable traits and lives of their own, are conspicuously absent from popular narratives. In fact, the absence of the mother is one of the most notable characteristics of contemporary children's entertainment. And nowhere is her absence more marked than in the phenomenally popular animated features produced by Walt Disney studios.

ABSENT MOTHERS, PLUCKY WOMEN, GOOD GIRLS

Beginning in the late eighties, Disney released a string of animated feature films based on fairy and folk tales — Hans Christian Andersen's *The Little Mermaid*, Charles Perrault's *Beauty and the Beast* and *Aladdin* from the Arabian Nights cycle. Each one has been more popular than the last, breaking box-office records and racking up unprecedented home video sales. These films, which kids today routinely watch dozens of times on home video, represent a return to Walt Disney's roots. His earliest forays into full-length animation — *Snow White, Cinderella, Sleeping Beauty* — were also based on fairy tales. "Uncle Walt" had a strong attraction to and feel for the fairy tale form, and it's interesting that the ones he gravitated to were largely female-centred stories. This isn't really surprising, because in contrast to the epic or quest tale, the fairy tale is the one traditional narrative form that often deals with female concerns and female experience. The older Disney features have been roundly criticized for sanitizing and sentimentalizing their raw folk sources, but the same criticism can be leveled at Perrault and the Grimm brothers who, like Disney, re-wrote and popularized fairy tales. Nowadays Disney's versions have also fallen into disrepute for their stereotyped portrayal of women — their evil stepmothers and airhead princesses waiting for their princes to come.

But Disney's genius lay not only in his pioneering animation and the narrative strength of his stories, but in his uncanny ability to put his finger on the popular pulse. For all their stereotypes, the Disney features are a fascinating barometer of images of women and the effect that feminism has had on them. The heroines of the contemporary features — Ariel in *Little Mermaid*, Belle in *Beauty and the Beast* and Princess Jasmine in *Aladdin* — are all clearly a response to contemporary feminism. They're "plucky," far more assertive than the old Disney heroines. Belle is a voracious reader of books who wants to escape the confines of her provincial small town. Princess Jasmine defies her father's attempt to marry her off to suitors she doesn't love. But all three share something else: the fact that they are motherless, that they are all being raised by kindly, though ineffectual, fathers. In these recent Disney features, the old negative stepmother image has been replaced by a void, and, to my mind, this isn't necessarily an improvement. By killing off the mother before the story even begins, these films subtly suggest that the relationship with the father, not the mother, is the primary one. These heroines are strictly their fathers' daughters. They draw what strength they have from men, not from other women. These modern, plucky young women are still cut off from the most important part of their female legacy, their models of female power. But the Disney features only reflect a much larger void in contemporary pop culture, which avoids the mother-daughter relationship like the plague. The success of films like *Joy Luck Club* and *Postcards from the Edge*, both of which explore the passionate ambivalence of the mother-daughter relationship, is heartening but still very much the exception. More recently, the movie sequel *My Girl 2* actually depicted a young girl on a quest for her female roots as she researches a school project about her own mother, who died when she was a baby. Unfortunately but not surprisingly, *My Girl 2* performed poorly at the box office.

Of the three Disney heroines, Belle in *Beauty and the Beast* is in many ways the most liberated. She isn't nearly as isolated from other women as Ariel and Princess Jasmine. From the beginning of her imprisonment in the Beast's castle, she receives deep emotional support from two very female confidantes, Mrs. Potts, the teapot, and her friend, the Wardrobe. And whether Disney executives really intended it as such, *Beauty and the Beast* is actually quite a sophisticated exposé of the ugly reality of male violence. Not too far beneath the surface of the broad caricature of the egocentric Gaston lies his abusiveness and need for total control over women. In fact, the true subject of *Beauty and the Beast* is the rehabilitation and redemption of another abusive male — the Beast. In that sense it's really his story, not Belle's. She's so good to begin with that her character has nowhere to go. We know from the start that she's too nice a person not to see through the Beast's harsh facade. His character is the one who grows and changes. The moment the Beast becomes aware that if he truly loves Belle, he must relinquish his need for control and give her her freedom, is a tremendously moving one. We see him finally accepting responsibility for his abusive behaviour, both towards Belle and the old witch he scorns at the beginning of the story. The Beast can no longer avoid the fact that he must grow up and learn to control his violent impulses.

One problem with the recent Disney features is that, for all that their heroines are a genuine improvement, they're still afflicted with terminal blandness. Their lack of definition, of sharp outlines, their too-goodness almost make one nostalgic for the glorious Disney villainesses of *Snow White*, *Cinderella* and *Sleeping Beauty*. Disney shamelessly sentimentalized the heroines of these films but not their evil adversaries. The wicked Queen, the stepmother, the evil fairy are at least allowed the full dignity and power of their evilness. It may be that the real task for feminists is not to eliminate stereotypes, but to free ourselves to be bad girls. The pressure to be good, to be "nice," to deny our own needs and desires and take care of others may be the greatest form of tyranny women face. In *Centuries of Childhood*, Philippe Ariès describes how through much of Western history girls have been expected to grow up earlier than boys. Traditionally girls had to leave behind the impulsiveness and self-centredness of childhood to assume adult responsibilities, while boys were expected to sow their wild oats. Several decades of twentieth-century feminism have

made little difference in this attitude. In many ways, feminists have contributed to it. In our zeal to eliminate stereotypes, we've come to demand only positive female role models. The problem is that too often we end up with bland,
bloodless characters and the same old dilemma: women are
still being allowed too narrow a range of behaviours and characteristics.

The popular 1984 film *The Neverending Story* is a good
example of this tyranny of the good girl. The ruler of
Fantasia, the land to which the young hero goes on his quest,
is a female, the Empress. But she is so ethereally, insipidly
sweet, so lacking in any visible power or charisma it's hard to
imagine her coaching a badminton team, much less ruling a
kingdom. Though the writers obviously intended the
Empress as a nod to enlightened gender attitudes, the film
basically gives the same old message: females are allowed to
be, not do, to stand for something, to serve as the object of
the male quest, but not to assert any power or initiative of
their own. The tendency in many popular children's entertainments these days is to give female characters a bit more
prominence, perhaps making the hero's sidekick a girl and
assigning her some non-stereotypical attribute like athletic
ability. The producers then feel their work is done, pleased
that they've demonstrated their enlightened attitudes. But all
too often these characters end up still passive, still reacting to
the hero rather than driving the action of the story in any significant way. The 1993 TV series *The Odyssey* was built
around the intriguing concept of a "Downworld" realm populated and ruled entirely by children. But the producers of
this much-praised series opted for the familiar son-in-search-
of-the-father quest, throwing in a girl-sidekick (who is also
disabled) and a smattering of "tough" minor female characters throughout the story.

The real problem is still fear of the powerful female.
We're seeing a lot more of the plucky woman these days, but

she's just not good enough. Her power is too circumscribed, her range too narrow. She still usually has to be rescued by the hero, and rarely does she get to command centre stage in the story. It's instructive in this regard to take a look at *Star Trek*, arguably the TV series that has done most to shatter stereotypes and showcase strong women characters. In its various incarnations over the past three decades, *Star Trek* has served as a barometer of the way attitudes towards strong women characters have evolved. The original series, with its female starship personnel flouncing around in micro-minis looks laughably sexist to us now, but it did have one woman officer, Lt. Uhura, who was black as well. What is little known outside Trek circles is that in the series' original pilot episode, the second-in-command on the Enterprise was female (played, as serious devotees know, by Majel Barrett, who later married series creator Gene Roddenberry). The network rejected the first pilot on the grounds that viewers wouldn't accept a woman with such senior rank. Subsequently Mr. Spock became second-in-command and Majel Barrett was demoted — to ship's nurse! Only now, after nearly 30 years, six feature films and *The Next Generation* TV series, has *Star Trek* finally acquired a female second-in-command — the Bajoran Major Kira Nerys in the *Deep Space Nine* series launched in early 1993. (And the saga continues. In the fall of 1994, the producers confirmed rumours that yet another spinoff series, *Star Trek: Voyager*, would debut in 1995 with — at long last — a female captain at the helm.)

Still, cracks in the prohibition against strong women sometimes turn up in unexpected corners of pop culture. While Arnold Schwarzenegger vehicles like *Kindergarten Cop* and *Terminator 2* have come under harsh criticism from antiviolence groups, hardly anyone has noted the fact that both these films feature tough-as-nails female characters who more than hold their own with Arnie. There is a harrowing scene in *Terminator 2: Judgement Day* where Sarah Connor (played by

Linda Hamilton) attacks the psychiatrist who is keeping her incarcerated. We seldom see women in the movies exhibiting the kind of naked rage Connor does in this scene. In our culture the sight of an angry woman is for many people more genuinely terrifying than all the high-tech weaponry of the *Terminator* films put together.

Kindergarten Cop turns one of the action genre's chief conventions on its head when Schwarzenegger is cornered and has to be rescued in the final shoot-out by his female partner, played by Pamela Reed. The film also has a running joke about Reed's character's formidable appetite. In this age of obsessive dieting and rampant female anorexia, *Kindergarten Cop* gives us a strong woman character whose power appears to be linked to the fact that she unabashedly feeds herself. Interestingly, in both movies Schwarzenegger plays a kind of killing machine who is humanized by his contact with children. And despite all the criticism leveled against them, both films also carry overt anti-violence messages. This kind of phenomenon — a movie that showcases a multitude of violent scenes, yet seems to argue against violence — seems inherently contradictory, but it's the kind of mixed message in which pop culture abounds.

ONLY THE LEADING ROLE WILL DO

The Appalachian folksinger Ola Belle Reed wrote a song some years ago called "Only the Leading Role Will Do." The song was the lament of a woman whose man is fooling around on her. She refuses to share his affections with other women any longer, saying she wants to be his one and only: "I can't play the supporting role in the story of your heart. Only the leading role will do." The irony, of course, is that women are starting to apply her ultimatum in a whole different way. We're no longer content to play supporting roles in men's stories, no matter how important or juicy, how offbeat or spunky those roles are. We don't want to be the Other. We want to see ourselves at the centre of the story. Only the lead-ing role will do.

But there are some major obstacles to the development of more female-centred narratives. One obstacle I pointed to ear-lier is the fact that stories about women's experience, with women protagonists, are presumed to be of interest only to women. They aren't perceived to be of general interest, that is, of interest to men as well. This is, at least in part, sheer preju-dice, stemming from the fundamental devaluing of things female that pervades our culture. But it also could have some-thing to do with the things women themselves choose to write about. In an article in *This Magazine* some years back, poet Paulette Jiles lamented the fact that so many women writers confine themselves to what she termed the "relationship novel." These kinds of stories, often written in what reviewers like to call "dense, lyrical" prose, focus almost entirely on the heroine's interior states of emotion and the minutiae of her relationships — chiefly with men but also with children, par-ents and other women. At its worst, Jiles says, the relationship novel degenerates into the "dependency melodrama":

> ... where it is *de rigueur* that the protagonist fall about in "feminine" stereotypes. To wit: passive, clinging, without purpose, timid, deferential, with no sense of herself outside of relatedness. All action must be given to the male charac-ters. Or evil women. She must also be attractive, and with-out any negative personality characteristics. Sound famil-iar? This is the heroine of Harlequin novels as well as much of what is passing for 'serious literature' written by women.

As Jiles points out, "Women have always had experiences other than those of relating. Why are we ignoring them in our fiction?" She calls for women writers to break out of the con-fines of the relationship novel and move into genres like the picaresque, which allow female protagonists to act as well as feel, to drive the story's engine rather than simply react to what other characters say and do. But in her analysis, Jiles puts her finger on an underlying problem: women also see themselves this way. Even when we put ourselves at the centre and take the leading role, we often subtly undermine ourselves and shift the focus to the other characters, usually the male lover. We give the more active stuff, the funny lines to the guys. Even when we're supposedly in the driver's seat, we're still the Other, even to ourselves.

This dynamic crops up again and again in recent movies. Take *Mermaids*, a 1990 vehicle for Cher, written by a female screenwriter and based on a novel by a woman writer. Cher's character, Mrs. Flax, is the protagonist — a sexy single mother who thumbs her nose at the conventions of the early sixties, in which the story is set. But much of the viewer's interest is subtly drawn to the boyfriend character played by Bob Hoskins. He is permitted to want things — marriage to Mrs. Flax, a chance to touch Lou Gehrig's glove — and spends the movie doing what he can to get them. But the film-makers don't allow Mrs. Flax anything more than a vague desire for "freedom," and since she doesn't want anything very specific, all that is left for her to do is react to what the other characters want of her. So she spends most of the movie saying "No" in one way or another — to Hoskins and to her children, who want a more normal family life. For all Cher's off-beat flamboyance, at the heart of this story there is a vacuum where a character should reside.

We seem to be suffering from a failure of imagination, a failure that is actually quite understandable given the dearth of images of active heroines we have to draw on. Herein lies an even deeper obstacle to female-centred narratives. As critic Carolyn Heilbrun writes, "One cannot make up stories: one can only retell in new ways the stories one has already heard." According to Heilbrun, the female-centred narrative is still largely an "as-yet-unwritten story: how a woman may manage her own destiny when she has no plot, no narrative, no tale to guide her." Like Penelope in the Odyssey, women are "without story," because we have been restricted to only one plot, which Heilbrun variously describes as "the marriage plot, the erotic plot, the courtship plot." As she says:

> Within the quest plot, men might do anything: literature tells us all they have done. Within the marriage plot women might only wait to be desired, to be wed, to be forgotten ...1. The question women must all ask is how to be freed from the marriage plot and initiated into the quest plot. How may women today find a script, a narrative, a story to live by?

So the problem facing women writers (and male writers who are tired of telling the same old stories) is how to move beyond the existing configurations, how to break down the old formulas and reshuffle them into some genuinely new stories with fresh insights about men and women, boys and girls. But why do they matter, these new stories? Why is it important that women and girls see images of female strength and narratives that put them at the centre?

The work of Carol Gilligan and Lyn Mikel Brown sheds some light on the question. In their recent study of girls on the threshold of adolescence, Gilligan and Brown found that this period is typically associated with a process of silencing, a "loss of voice." As they moved through the years from 8 to 13, the girls in this study showed more and more of a tendency to refrain from speaking and acting on their own behalf, to put the needs and feelings of others ahead of their own. Eleven- and twelve-year-old girls, who had been so confident in their opinions and forthright in expressing them in interviews a year or two earlier, gradually learned to censor their behaviour and even their thoughts in order to mould themselves into the image of the "good girl" who is always loving and caring, who puts aside her own feelings to tend to others. Gilligan and Brown variously describe this process as a "wound" and a kind of "psychological foot-binding." They suggest that it may represent a developmental crisis comparable to the "Oedipal scar" experienced by boys in early child-hood. Perhaps their most distressing finding is that "it was the adult women in their lives that provided the models for silencing themselves and behaving like 'good little girls'." Far more than boys, girls are praised by mothers and teachers for being co-operative, for smoothing over conflicts and being sensitive to the needs of others — for, in essence, losing themselves.

Gilligan and Brown's work documents the inner processes that take place as girls move out of Girl Culture, the female-centred, all-girl world they inhabit as young children. As they move into adolescence, the girls in their study are having greater and greater difficulty holding on to their own voices, telling their own story and putting themselves at the centre of it. Like the women characters Paulette Jiles describes in her discussion of relationship novels, their inner lives are increasingly consumed with anticipating and reacting to the feelings of others. At this same point in their lives, girls feel the pressure to disconnect from each other, to replace the primary girl-to-girl bonds of childhood with a focus on relationships with boys. They increasingly become reflections of Ariel the Mermaid, April O'Neill and all those motherless girls lacking any visible bonds with other females. All too often, the bonds they do have with women are telling them to be good, to be "nice," rather than to be strong, to take care of others rather than to look after themselves.

But let's not be too hard on these adult women. Let's face it: They R Us. We are passing on the only woman's story we know, because, as Carolyn Heilbrun says, the new narratives for women still remain to be written. But they are emerging, often in hard-to-recognize forms and unexpected places.

CHAPTER FIVE

New Stories: Girlfriends and Girl-Heroes

THE PREVIOUS CHAPTER is a lament for the great hole in our culture where women's stories ought to be. But I'm not really as pessimistic is much of that discussion may have sounded; I think the hole is beginning to be filled. This chapter, and indeed much of the rest of this book, is a celebration of the "new stories" — about woman protagonists and women's experiences — which I see emerging more and more in popular culture. But before I launch into that discussion, I think it's important to look at some of the older stories and narrative traditions from which these new stories spring. For the roots of many of these stories are to be found in an ancient, largely female-centred narrative tradition, though it's not often recognized as such: folk and fairy tales.

Like many of the things now considered fit only for children, fairy tales used to be for adults, too. They were once part of a great common folk culture that included the rhymes and circle dances I discussed in Chapter Two and that the whole community enjoyed and took part in. But the modern age has consigned the fairy tale, with its magical elements and deceptive simplicity, to the realm of childhood (though we now seem to be coming full circle, with the renewed interest in fairy tales inspired by Jungian psychology and the popularity of books like Robert Bly's *Iron John* and Clarissa Pinkola Estés' *Women Who Run with the Wolves*, which draw on fairy tale themes for personal growth). Like fairy tales, women also tend to be considered "childish," so it's not too surprising that fairy tales are, by and large, a women's genre. The epic or myth, as we saw in the previous chapter, is in most cultures an exclusively male-oriented genre, concentrating on action and warfare, and the larger-than-life epic hero is almost universally male. But fairy tales, as Bruno Bettelheim points out, are much more "homely" and down-to-earth. Though they usually have supernatural elements, they are less about slaying mythical beasts and performing superhuman feats than they are about dealing with the ordinary dilemmas and sorrows of human living — rejection, loneliness, feeling unworthy. In a sense, fairy tales take place more in the "domestic" realm — the realm of family and relationships — than do myths. And, though women's experiences and interests have little value in the larger society, the domestic realm is the one place where these things are valued, where they take centre stage.

But the prominence of the love story, Heilbrun's "courtship plot," in so many of the best-known fairy tales has posed a problem for feminists. Our impulse is to dismiss them as stereotypes, dated products of an older, irretrievably sexist period that have no place in modern society. Fairy tales such as *Snow White* and *Cinderella* seem to convey the message that a woman's main goal in life is to find and marry her prince, that she can find completion and fulfillment only in a man. There have been efforts in the past decade to unearth alternatives to these tales in the existing folk traditions, especially "plucky women" tales in which women characters take initiative and have the kind of adventures traditionally reserved for male characters. This is a worthy effort but it shouldn't lead us to throw the baby out with the bath water and dismiss the romantic fairy tale out of hand. The fairy tale, after all, is a narrative form in which female protagonists are the rule, rather than the exception. *Snow White* and *Cinderella* are named after their main characters, who are female. In these tales it's the princes who play the subsidiary "love interest" role, who are vague personages, even without names of their own.

The "passivity" we see in these fairy tale heroines isn't necessarily an accurate reflection of their origins. Most of us are familiar with these tales through the classic Walt Disney films. For better or worse, we've made Disney our storyteller. For all his popular genius in bringing these tales to a wider audience at a time when interest in them was on the wane, there's no denying their heroines were shortchanged by the process of Disneyfication. There's no suggestion in the Brothers Grimm's original version of "Cinderella" — *Aschenputtel* — that Cinderella is pining away waiting for any prince to come. Throughout the tale, in fact, her deepest longing is for her dead mother. Disney, of course, was just one of a long line of re-interpreters, including Charles Perrault and the Grimm brothers themselves, who freely altered the tales from their original form when they set them down on paper. And "original form" is itself a misnomer, since nothing in folk traditions has a fixed form. Fairy tales, like folk songs, may appear in a variety of versions, even within the same cultural group. Disney's sin, such as it was, was not so much in altering the tales but in the stamp of passivity and blandness his versions leave on the heroines.

Feminists are just as bothered by Disney's evil queens and stepmothers, but in this he was at least true to the fairy tale tradition, which abounds in these archetypes. What feminist criticisms tend to ignore, however, is the tremendous power of these evil female figures. Disney's heroines may be trivialized, but his evil queens certainly are not. They have truly awesome and frightening power over life and death, and they use it unabashedly. This is also true to the fairy tale tradition, which doesn't deny the enormous power of women, especially of the mother, for good or evil. Fairy tales deal with this power in much the same way children's psyches do: They attempt to preserve the image of the good mother by displacing all her negative power onto a replacement — an evil stepmother or fairy godmother. This is not "realistic" — real-life mothers, like all human beings, are a mix of good and bad — but it isn't meant to be realistic.

For all the so-called negative images of women in fairy tales, female power commands respect, and the bonds between women are not only strongly present, but are taken seriously. Though the good mother has often died before or soon after the tale begins, she is seldom completely absent, as she is in the Disney films. A major theme in many of the well-known tales is the mother's gift to her daughter of power, wisdom and healing, a gift that reverberates long after her death. In *The Goose Girl*, this gift is a white handkerchief with three drops of the mother's blood. In many versions of *Cinderella*, Cinderella's wishes are granted not by some generic fairy godmother who appears out of the ether, as in Disney's version, but by a white bird that lights in the hazel bush growing over her mother's grave.

Cinderella is a good example of a fairy tale that has taken an undeserved bad rap for sexism. This tale, which survives in an enormous number of versions in various cultures, has resonances far beyond what our modern superficial view of it as a mere love story would suggest. Bruno Bettelheim regarded it as a symbolic exploration of some of the deepest anxieties of childhood — the intense love/hate feelings between siblings, the fear of being the unloved outcast. The evil stepmother and stepsisters may be thorns in the side of modern feminists, but the tale's antecedents are just as hard, if not harder, on Cinderella's father. In fact, Bettelheim quotes a cross-cultural survey of "Cinderella" stories in his *The Uses of Enchantment*, which reveals that in many versions, the real cause of

Cinderella's misery is not only a cruel stepmother but a "father who wants to marry his daughter." Confirmed Freudian that he is, Bettelheim sees this as the daughter's "oedipal attachment" to her father. But it's just as likely that it's the father who wants her, that the none-too-subtle subtext of this cycle of tales is the prevalence of incest in many cultures. The true subject of "Cinderella" may be not the fair maiden hoping for true love, but the daughter trying to escape a sexually abusive father. In this reading, the dead mother whose love can only be felt spiritually makes even more sense, because so often the daughter finds that the living mother lets her down and is unwilling or unable to protect her from the abuse. In some cases, the living mother, like the evil stepmother, may even be abusive herself. So these tales do not gloss over the mother's failings, but in the symbolism of the dead mother's gifts, they also keep alive the hope that good mothering and good parenting do exist. The ashes or cinders to which Cinderella is consigned also take on a much deeper meaning, for they symbolize the total isolation of the abused child, who blames herself and feels she must guard the terrible family secret at all costs. It's not surprising that these elements have been downplayed or suppressed altogether in modern fairy tale retellings, because they carry some of the harsh truths about the patriarchal family we are only now beginning to face up to.

Other tales that appear sexist on the surface are actually telling important truths about women's lives. There are a number of tales like *The Goose Girl* and *The Six Swans* in which the protagonist is forbidden to speak for a prolonged period of time, under pain of her own or someone else's death. These tales bear eloquent witness to the demands placed on women through the ages to be silent and self-sacrificing. *The Six Swans* belongs to a group of tales in which a girl is born into a family of many brothers who are transformed into swans or ravens. In all of them it is the girl who is the active agent, who goes out into the world, usually utterly alone, and submits to a series of trials or tests in order to redeem her brothers. In these tales it is the brothers who must wait passively to be rescued. It's interesting, too, that in this cycle of tales, it's usually the daughter who is the treasured offspring and the sons who are disparaged.

Sex roles are much more fluid in the fairy tale universe than we've been led to think. There are many examples of tales in which a role played by a male character is played by a female character in another version. The "animal groom" cycle of fairy tales, in which a human is transformed into an animal or beast and redeemed by true love, includes some of the best-known examples of this. In the Grimms' *The Frog King*, a prince undergoes transformation into a frog, while in many Slavic versions of the tale, the enchanted frog turns out to be a princess. There are also abundant examples, even in well-known tales, of females who, far from needing to be rescued, are decisive and even ruthless. In *The Frog King*, it is the princess's rage, far more than her love, that finally redeems the prince. Fed up with the frog's endless demands, the princess flings him against a wall, whereupon he is promptly changed back to his human self. And it's often overlooked that the apparently meek and fearful Gretel in *Hansel and Gretel* is the one who finishes off the witch by pushing her into that hot oven.

Fairy tales are a repository for deep wells of folk wisdom accumulated over the centuries. Bettelheim argues that their endurance and continued relevance lie in the "existential dilemmas" they pose to children and adults. The fairy tale genre has such deep resonance for us that, beginning in the nineteenth century, writers began trying to write "original" or literary fairy tales, with varying degrees of success. Lewis Carroll's *Alice in Wonderland* and *Through the Looking Glass* are probably the most familiar examples of literary fairy tales from this period. Another popular nineteenth-century children's writer, George MacDonald, produced a series of novels that consciously drew on fairy tale motifs, the best known of which is *The Princess and the Goblin*. True to the fairy tale tradition, these authors put female characters at the centre of their stories and did not shrink from portraying female power in both its positive and negative aspects. Contemporary children's authors have also produced stories that strive for the depth and timeless feel of traditional fairy tales. One of the more successful attempts is Peter S. Beagle's *The Last Unicorn*, which was made into an animated feature film in 1982. Beagle's story draws on familiar fairy tale conventions but with some interesting and decidedly modern twists. This time, the animal transformation goes the other way, as the Unicorn is changed into the beautiful Lady Amalthea, then back to her original animal form at the story's climax. The fairy tale romance plot also undergoes a reversal: somewhat reminiscent of a juvenile version of Casablanca, the story closes with the unicorn choosing her higher purpose — to free her sister unicorns — over her love for Prince Lear. The major theme of *The Last Unicorn* is one that is emerging more and more in contemporary female-centred stories: the crumbling of the patriarch's "false" power and the release of the female power he has held captive over the centuries. This theme is gradually acquiring the status of a modern myth, and its first clearly articulated expression was in a would-be "anti-fairy tale" published at the turn of this century.

OZ: A FEMALE MYTH

The Wizard of Oz is generally thought of, even by many of its strongest devotees, as a story about a sweet young girl catapulted by a tornado to a beautiful, Eden-like place where she inexplicably spends all her time trying to figure out how to get back home to the grim Kansas prairie. It's seen as charming, but certainly not as a story that makes large statements or breaks any kind of new ground. But the publication of

L. Frank Baum's *The Wonderful Wizard of Oz* (the book's original title — the "wonderful" was dropped in subsequent editions) in 1900 was a breakthrough in female-centred narrative. It is the first — perhaps still the only — epic with a female hero, a story that has had an incalculable impact on other female-centred stories, on genres such as fantasy and science fiction, and on popular culture as a whole.

Oz and its many sequels never gained much in the way of literary respectability. Baum was for a long time considered little more than a hack writer. Because of their reliance on fantasy and magic, the *Oz* books were denounced by some experts as "unwholesome" and many librarians refused to stock them. That may have been just as well, because *Oz* did an end run around the literati via the movies, thereby achieving its true destiny as a popular myth. The 1939 movie version of *The Wizard of Oz* was a quintessential product of the Hollywood studio system, worked and reworked by no fewer than ten different screenwriters. (There were earlier, silent film renditions of the *Oz* stories, several of them produced by Baum himself.) And like most book-to-film adaptations, it has been the subject of much debate. Whatever damage the film may have done to the original story, as some of the book's devotees claim, it seems clear that *Oz* would not have become one of the signature myths of our century had not the medium of film taken the images of the twister, the yellow brick road and the Witch's hourglass and made them larger than life.

The character of Dorothy was originally based on a beloved niece of Baum's. Despite the fact that her creator and most of the screenwriters were male, Dorothy's journey is a peculiarly female one, abounding in female symbolism and the issues and conflicts that define the lives of women and girls. One of Baum's stated aims in the original story was to revive the archetype of the Good Witch. There are, of course, many of these benevolent figures in the fairy tale tradition, as well as other, more ambivalent figures like the Slavic Baba Yaga, whose apparent cruelty brings about good outcomes. But witches and sorceresses have had a very bad press since the days of the Inquisition, and the fairy tales popularized by Walt Disney all feature powerful female figures who are unrelentingly evil. Baum tried to restore some balance to the Witch archetype by inventing a whole quartet of witches for the land of Oz — two "good" (of the North and South) and two "bad" witches (of the East and West). He makes clear his intentions in Dorothy's first encounter with the Witch of the North, when she protests, "I thought all witches were wicked." The Good Witch immediately sets her straight: "Oh, no, that is a great mistake," and she goes on to inform Dorothy that witches and wizards still exist in Oz because, unlike Kansas, "the Land of *Oz* has never been civilized." Baum's *Oz* appears to be situated in pre-Christian territory, with echoes of pagan magic and goddess worship.

To some extent the film undercuts Baum's intent by focusing so strongly on the Wicked Witch of the West. Certainly she is the character we react to most strongly, the one who stays with us long after the film is over, despite the astonishing fact that she is on the screen for a total of only 12 minutes. Generations of adults can vividly recall, decades after first seeing the film, the utter terror they felt hearing the Witch's maniacal laugh as her face obliterates the image of Aunt Em in the crystal ball. It also doesn't much help that the Good Witch Glinda is so saccharine and bland. But whatever else we might say about *Oz*'s witches, both good and evil, at least they all have some measure of real power, which is more than can be said of the empty figurehead Wizard. Baum's original story is actually a fascinating meditation on the whole notion of power, a theme that survives fairly intact in the film. In *Oz*, it is the (female) witches who are powerful, but they labour — as does everyone else — under the misconception that the (male) Wizard is, in the Witch of the

North's words, "more powerful than all the rest of us together."
Dorothy similarly underestimates her own power: "You are a
great Wizard, and I am only a helpless little girl," she says at
her first encounter with the Great and Powerful Oz. But the
whole progress of Dorothy's journey is her discovery that the
very things she believes herself incapable of doing — killing
the Wicked Witch, restoring peace and order to Oz, getting
back to Kansas — she is in fact eminently capable of doing.
Inside this rather timid girl there is a much more powerful
one bursting to get out. This is a key point in seeing Baum's
story as the radical departure that it is — an epic with a
female hero that acknowledges and celebrates female power,
rather than relegating it to the margins and shadows.

Unfortunately, this theme is severely undercut by the
film's portrayal of Dorothy, and it is Judy Garland's luminous
Dorothy, not Baum's, that is so vividly etched in our minds.
Actually, there isn't a vast difference between the two. Baum's
Dorothy is unfailingly sweet-natured and polite, and, like
Garland's, goes to great pains not to cause trouble or harm to
anyone — the quintessential Good Girl. But the film takes
two story elements — Dorothy's melting the Witch with the
bucket of water and her desire to return home — and alters
them subtly from the book, with the overall effect of magnify-
ing Dorothy's timidity and cravenness. For example, in both
film and book, Dorothy apologizes to the Witch as she watches her melt away. But in Baum's version she tosses the bucket
of water deliberately and in anger. In the film, she douses the
Witch by accident as she tries to put out a fire in the
Scarecrow's straw. To add insult to injury, the screenwriters
have her blubber her apologies over and over to the Witch's
guards. To be fair to the film, though, this is all too typical of
the way girls and women actually do behave in those
moments when they act, when they claim power, especially
when it involves causing harm to other people. As Carol
Gilligan's work shows, the desire to avoid inflicting hurt is an

over-riding theme permeating girls' behaviour and women's morality. Nevertheless, the film-makers seem to go out of their way to underscore Dorothy's reluctance to exercise or claim power, most notably in the film's closing moments when she vows that "if I ever go looking for my heart's desire again, I won't look any further than my own backyard." It would be unthinkable to put these words into the mouth of a male protagonist. Furthermore, such a sentiment appears nowhere in the original, which closes only with Dorothy's avowal to Aunt Em that she's "so glad to be at home again." I don't want to suggest that Dorothy's oft-expressed desire to go back to Kansas is inherently sexist. After all, even Odysseus was trying to get home; it's the heartfelt desire of all epic heroes. But Dorothy's closing lines go further and suggest that her whole adventure, the things she's learned and the personal power she's gained, have all been a big mistake. Good girls should stay home where they belong.

Other departures from the original have more positive effects. For example, the fact that the film-makers have Dorothy's journey to Oz take place in a dream rather than in waking reality has caused much consternation among the book's fans over the years. But to me, this doesn't really undercut the power of Dorothy's quest. All true myth unfolds in a kind of dream time, where magic holds sway and the distinctions between "real" and "imaginary" are necessarily blurred. Another change in the film was the transformation of the Wicked Witch of the East's magic shoes — which are silver in the book — into the famous gleaming, sequin-studded ruby slippers. The reason for this change has remained something of a mystery. It's generally attributed to the principal screenwriter, Noel Langley, but no apparent motive for the change has ever surfaced in the extensive lore surrounding the film's creation. Possibly Langley's share of the collective unconscious was working overtime when he wrote it in, because red is a powerful colour with ancient female associations of blood, rage and sexuality. With the strong visual statement they make in the film, the ruby slippers help restore, thematically at least, some of Dorothy's thwarted anger and power.

Is *Oz* a myth or fairy tale? Baum himself regarded his creation as "a modernized fairy tale, in which the wonderment and joy are retained and the heart-aches and nightmares left out." While it's debatable whether he achieved the latter — the book, and certainly the film, abound in the conflicts and fears of childhood — "fairy tale" is certainly the way most people would characterize the story. It has the magical events and requisite happy "fairy tale" ending. Dorothy's quirkily memorable trio of companions are certainly reminiscent of the gnomes, helpful animals and other not-quite-human denizens of the fairy tale universe. As they do in the Jungian view of fairy tales, these characters serve a key symbolic function in representing the challenges and qualities the hero must master in order to become whole. Perhaps most tellingly, *Oz* strikes us as a fairy tale because we think of it primarily as a children's story. But when MGM studios set out to film Baum's book, there was no suggestion that it was aimed particularly at children, though it was certainly meant to be a family entertainment. This was despite the fact that the story had a child protagonist and magical elements. Of course, the child was played by the nearly adult Judy Garland and was live action, not animated like Disney's classic fairy tale treatments.

In my view, *Oz* is an unusual, possibly unique hybrid of fairy tale and myth. It has the down-to-earth air of a fairy tale in its characters' relationships and their childlike naivete. But their journey has an epic quality and scope. Unlike most fairy tales, there's no love story, no courtship plot in *The Wizard of Oz*. It is, at bottom, a quest tale, and it tackles the large themes associated with that form. The great subject of *Oz* is the disintegration of the patriarchy and the ascendancy of female power, and the film is particularly prophetic in its depiction of how this "false" power is perpetuated in modern times through media manipulation of images. The Wizard makes himself appear more powerful than he is by projecting the image of his head onto an enormous screen, an uncanny forerunner of the talking heads that populate television, a medium then in its infancy.

Oz also anticipated many of the major themes and motifs of modern science fiction. There is an abundance of characters in the *Oz* books who are some combination of organic and mechanical, human and man-made. The Tin Woodman, TikTok and the Wheelers all anticipate the robots and androids of sci-fi. Characters like TikTok and the Scarecrow are spiritual fathers to Data of *Star Trek* — all man-made creatures who long to become fully human. The *Star Trek* connection is particularly apt, because *Oz* has become a modern myth in much the same way as the popular TV series. Both *Oz* and *Star Trek* have evolved into alternate, endlessly expanding universes, largely a result of pressure from devotees. Baum was hounded by his readers to keep churning out sequels to the original *Oz* story. And it was the fanatical devotion of *Star Trek* fans that returned the series to the airwaves after its initial cancellation and that ultimately gave rise to the series of feature films, *The Next Generation* TV series and the latest spin-off, *Deep Space Nine*. Just as the sci-fi series keeps generating new characters and stories, the characters and symbols of *Oz* have been endlessly recycled. The major symbols of *Oz*, such as the Emerald City and the Yellow Brick Road, have become so embedded in North American culture they may be rivaled in familiarity only by the Bible and Shakespeare.

Another aspect of *Oz*'s mythic status is its ability to accommodate an enormous range of meanings and interpretations. Alison Lurie sees the film as a gigantic metaphor for the Hollywood Dream Factory. To Aljean Harmetz, author of

The Making of the Wizard of Oz, the film's themes of home-coming and "Over the Rainbow" struck chords of deep longing in the war-torn world of the late thirties. *Oz* has been inter-preted as an elaborate political allegory of American capital-ism, populism and monetary policy. Psychotherapist Evelyn Bassoff has written about *Oz* as a healing myth for women in recovery from deprived and abused childhoods. Partly due to the presence of Judy Garland, it has even become a gay cult film of sorts. *Oz* has the apparent ability to be all things to all people, containing all these interpretations and more, quite comfortably. Like any true myth, its potential meanings are inexhaustible. It is far more than the sum of its parts.

But it's *Oz*'s role as a specifically female-centred myth and the fact that it laid the groundwork for new female narratives in popular culture that interests us here. So strong is the female focus in the *Oz* cycle that in the one instance in the series in which Dorothy is replaced by a male protagonist — Tip in *The Marvellous Land of Oz* — he undergoes a sex change! In true fairy tale tradition, Tip is revealed near the end of the book to have been under a witch's spell since baby-hood, having been transformed into a boy. The spell is lifted by none other than our old friend the Good Witch Glinda, and Tip is restored to his true form as Princess Ozma, long-lost heir to the throne of Oz. Again, all the real power in *Oz* proves to reside with the females. In this, the second book in the *Oz* series, we learn that the Wizard kidnapped Ozma in an attempt to seize control of Oz. But he has to go to the witch Mombi to hide her, which she does by casting the sex-changing spell on Ozma and keeping her captive as the boy Tip. Once Ozma is restored to her true self, she is acknowl-edged as the legitimate ruler of Oz and continues to reign through the rest of the series with an authority and wisdom never exhibited by the Wizard during his tenure.

Sex confusions are a recurring theme in the *Oz* stories. Dorothy's constant companion in the third book, replacing her dog Toto, is Billina, a hen who undergoes a sex change of sorts herself. "When I was first hatched," she tells Dorothy, "no one could tell whether I was going to be a hen or a rooster." So she was given the name Bill. "That's a boy's name," Dorothy protests and promptly changes the hen's name to the more feminine-sounding Billina. One signal of Billina's true nature is that she failed to make the grade as a rooster: "I didn't crow and fight, as all the roosters do." This is not unlike many of the male characters in the *Oz* cycle who, as psychoanalyst and *Oz* enthusiast Justin Call has noted, are "fractured, in some state of disrepair, incomplete in their anatomy." The Scarecrow lacks a brain, the Cowardly Lion courage. TikTok, the mechanical man of the later *Oz* books, can function only when a human winds up his mechanism. The Tin Woodman, whose harrowing story is not included in the film version, starts out as a flesh-and-blood woodcutter. But the Wicked Witch of the East casts a spell on his axe that makes him systematically chop off all his own body parts, which are replaced, one by one, with metal parts by the local tinsmith. And the Wizard, the "Great and Powerful Oz," turns out to be nothing but a "humbug," reduced to playing parlour tricks rather than exercising real power. Though many of the female characters in the *Oz* books are evil, like Mombi and the Wicked Witches, or vain and irresponsible like Princess Langwidere, none of them suffer from the kinds of wounds and deep-seated deficiencies that afflict so many of the males. In our world, of course, it is females who lack power; in Freudian psychology, it is females who are thought to be "incomplete in their anatomy." But in Baum's *Oz* stories the situation is reversed: it's the women who are complete and powerful. The men are no match for them.

TEEN DAUGHTERS OF OZ

The Wizard of Oz may have laid the groundwork for new female-centred narratives, but the intervening years haven't exactly produced a torrent of them. This is partly, as we've seen, because the men who control the popular culture industries aren't turned on by stories about women and often frankly admit they find them lacking in excitement. For the same reason, men and boys stay away from female-centred entertainments in droves, which only reinforces male producers' reluctance to produce them. But male resistance is only part of the problem. As Carolyn Heilbrun points out, new stories have to draw on the models of the old, and comparatively few models of female-centred narratives exist yet. Women and girls crave stories about female experience, but the creative impulse for these stories doesn't come out of thin air. Where will the models, the inspiration come from? It's a bit like the circular dilemma faced by young job-seekers, who are told they can't get a job without experience and can't get experience unless they have a job.

One surprisingly fertile ground for new stories about female experience is teen movies. These films have a built-in appeal for female audiences, with their focus on love stories, relationships and the trivia of high school life. (And "teen" is something of a misnomer, since a major portion of the audience for these films is pre-teen girls as young as seven or eight.) But they've tended to be dismissed in the same way so many other women's genres, from soap operas to romance novels to Archie comics, have been. But why should these genres, all built in varying degrees around love and romance, be considered any less valid than male-oriented genres like war movies and Westerns? The problem lies not with women's genres' focus on the courtship plot, but in the fact that women, as Heilbrun argues, have been "restricted to only one plot." We have been confined to one story, when in fact our lives have as wide a range of stories as men's. Women are now more and more moving to claim the quest plot, the leading roles, for ourselves. But this doesn't mean we should disown the courtship plot altogether.

For better or for worse, the powerful appeal of teen movies and magazines such as *Seventeen* for young women is largely due to their heavy emphasis on dating, romance and the other elements of the boy-meets-girl story. On one level, it's true, of course, that they help promulgate the sexist message that women can find completion in a relationship only with a man. But there are reasons that romance novels and love stories remain so enduringly popular even with "liberated" women. These forms seem to speak to some deeper longing in women and girls, one that I believe is more than just the desire to lose oneself in a man. Losing oneself, let's not forget, is also a spiritual state, and Jungians particularly see the search for the beloved as a quest for union with the divine here on earth. One great source of misunderstanding about romance stories, and fairy tales in general, is their ending with the finding of true love. Many people criticize the happy-ever-after ending as "unrealistic," but that's precisely the point. One of the functions of story is to take us beyond the realistic, beyond the constraints of this world. Because we live in such a spiritually impoverished culture, this function of narrative and myth is now grossly misunderstood. Instead of being celebrated for their ability to satisfy some of our deeper longings in fantasy, romances and fairy tales come under continual and unwarranted fire in the modern world for creating "unrealistic" hopes and expectations.

To add to all that, heterosexual romance is somewhat politically suspect these days, what with the widespread media focus on wife battering, sexual harassment and date rape. In the face of all this, though, young women and teenage girls persist in their reluctance to tar all male-female relationships with the same bleak brush, at a time in their lives when forming bonds with males is all-important. Older feminists may find their stance naive, but heterosexual young women want to believe that true love between the sexes is still possible. And on the evidence of some of the teen movies of recent years, they might be right.

Films such *Earth Girls Are Easy, Buffy the Vampire Slayer* and *Heathers* look on the surface like standard-issue frothy teen romances. But each of these films in its own way breaks out of the confines of the courtship plot while still retaining many of its most satisfying motifs and conventions. All three stories have female protagonists whose actions drive the narrative, who not only find true love, but take action and exercise power in the process. What some of the more interesting new teen movies are doing, by various methods and degrees, is claiming the heroic role for female characters and combining the traditional male quest plot with the courtship plot. In doing so, they're giving young women a startling new message: that they can be both heroes and lovers, just as men have always been allowed to be.

Earth Girls gave me one of my first and best lessons on the value of following kids' lead and trusting their taste. My nine-year-old daughter and her friends somehow discovered the film when it came out on video in 1990 after a not-very-successful run in theatres. Much to their mothers' dismay, they got together in gangs and watched the movie numerous times. On the face of it, our concerns seemed justified. This is a movie whose heroine is a manicurist whose life goals seem to be getting married and attending a Nail Expo, in that order. Valerie, played by Geena Davis, works in a garish southern California beauty salon, where the clientele launch into a surreal musical production number at the prospect of a beauty makeover. *Earth Girls* revels in its girliness, which is why it has such intense appeal for prepubescent girls who are too young to date but too old to play with Barbies. The whole film is, in fact, an ever so slightly more grown-up version of Barbie, taking place in a pastel world where girls can give themselves unabashedly over to their love of make-up, nail polish, new hairdoes.

The movie's plot is an ingenious inversion of *The Wizard of Oz*. Instead of Valerie going to *Oz* to meet her three oddball companions, they come to her in the form of three spectacularly hairy aliens, whose spaceship crash-lands in Valerie's backyard pool. She spends the movie trying to help them retrieve their vessel and keeping them out of the clutches of Ted, her knife-happy surgeon fiancé, who wants to dissect them and get his picture on the cover of *Time*. Once the trio has been subjected to hairstylist Candy's cutting shears ("I see split ends are universal"), Valerie naturally falls for the tallest, handsomest of them. Therein lies the movie's more genuinely serious purpose, however giddily expressed. For *Earth Girls* is a love story with a feminist subtext, a courtship plot that dictates that the woman be not the prize but the one who does the choosing. Valerie starts out suffering from a typically female brand of low self-esteem, blaming herself because her relationship with the shallow, self-centred, womanizing Ted isn't going well. "You're always trying to make Ted happy," her friend Candy tells her. "But who's making you happy?" Valerie's real task is to learn to put herself at the centre of her own life, to value her own needs and find a mate who's grown-up enough to accept that. It's the film's little feminist joke that she has to look to another species from an alien planet to find such a man.

Another of the film's delicious ironies is the fact that the woman who conceived the story and co-wrote the screenplay, Julie Brown (of MTV fame), also plays the movie's most "stereotyped" character, Candy. Her big production number at the beach, "'Cause I'm a Blonde," is a hilarious bimbo anthem, incorporating and sending up every known stereotype of the dumb blonde. *Earth Girls* is a modern fairy tale that lets girls enjoy being girls while poking fun at sexism and male self-importance at the same time. It also lets girls believe in the possibility of true love without denying the reality that so many men are jerks. Like the best fairy tales, it urges us to hold on to the dream, not to settle for less than true happiness.

Earth Girls situates itself squarely in the fairy tale tradition, but *Buffy the Vampire Slayer* is a teen movie that's more clearly moving into the quest genre. In fact, this 1992 film plays with many of the main conventions of Joseph Campbell's "hero monomyth." When Valley Girl cheerleader Buffy (played by Kristy Swanson) is "called" by an otherworldly mentor to fight vampires, like so many of her mythic forebears she tries to refuse. Despite her protests that she wants nothing more out of life than to shop till she drops, Buffy eventually submits and, like Campbell's mythic heroes, is put through a harrowing process of initiation to prepare her for the task of battling the vampires that are infiltrating her high school. Like *Earth Girls*, *Buffy* is a story of finding the true Mr. Right, the one who accepts and appreciates her for who she really is. The boyfriend in this case — Pike, played by Luke Perry — learns not only to accept Buffy's strength, but also sees that it's superior to his. He plays a decidedly supporting role, both in the movie and in Buffy's quest. It's her show and he knows it. Unlike *Earth Girls*, though, *Buffy* is not mainly a love story. The real subject of the film is Buffy's heroic quest and, more particularly, how she constantly moves back and forth between "male" and "female" modes of action to carry it out. Not that Buffy in any way has to "become a man" in order to be a vampire slayer. The film very explicitly links her emerging power with her femaleness, especially her menstrual cycle. "Great," she says to her mentor, Merrick, at one point. "My secret weapon is PMS." Images of redness, blood and power reminiscent of Dorothy's ruby slippers permeate the film, like the huge red bow on Buffy's prom dress. Even the physical system by which Buffy builds up her strength for combat is gymnastics, a quintessentially "girl" sport.

But it's also clear that in order to become a true warrior, Buffy must sometimes act like a man and muscle her way into male space, which she does most spectacularly when she confronts a vampire in the gym during the big basketball game. At this, the male players and spectators are fit to be tied, more outraged by this trespass violation ("There's a girl on the court!") than appreciative of her intervention. As in the *Oz* series, there are moments of sexual ambiguity and confusion in Buffy: "You're the guy, the chosen guy," Pike tells her at one point. At the height of the climactic vampire battle, Buffy dons Pike's black leather bomber jacket over her white prom dress. The film ends with the two lovers finally free to dance instead of having to fight vampires. But they are caught up in poignant confusion over which one should lead. Neither wants to, yet somehow they manage to keep on dancing, which is about as charming a way of getting the equality message across to young girls as I've seen in film.

It's also worth noting that the ending of Buffy is a conspicuous departure from more typical teen genre films like the *Prom Night* and *Nightmare on Elm Street* series. In these films, young women are titillatingly depicted as victims, not warriors, and most of the prom-goers end up dead, with the murderer or evil force still at large at the film's end (presumably to pave the way for the endless string of sequels these films generate). But there are signs that feminism is beginning to muscle its way into slasher films, too. Sara Risher, who produced a number of the *Elm Street* films, says she fought to have the Freddy Krueger character kill male as well as female characters. "That broke the rule in horror films," Risher claims, "in which the woman is always killed right after having sex, presumably as punishment for having it, and generally while she's not dressed."

Of recent girl-hero teen movies, *Heathers*, released in 1989, is probably the darkest in theme and tone. Though on the surface even more caught up with the minutiae of high school life than *Buffy*, *Heathers* breaks most clearly with the conventions of the teen movie, especially in its treatment of the love story. Like Buffy, the film's heroine Veronica, played by Winona Ryder, feels herself "called" to root out an evil influence in her high school. At first her goal is to stop the reign of terror by the school's trio of bitch-queens, all named Heather, and she's aided in this task by her new boyfriend, the cool, iconoclastic Jason Dean or J.D. But she naively gets drawn into a wave of "teen suicides" that are actually murders engineered by J.D., and she slowly comes to realize that he's the real enemy, the evil force that has to be stopped. This is a striking reversal of the courtship plot, which nevertheless mirrors real life for many women, who find their Prince Charming does indeed become a threat to them after the honeymoon is over. And its audacity is underscored by the fact that the budding serial killer is played with Nietzschean charm by teen idol Christian Slater. The film throws out a keen challenge to the adolescent romantic belief system when Veronica says this line as she shoots J.D. to keep him from blowing up the school and everyone in it: "You know what I want? Cool guys like you out of my life."

The complexity of *Heathers'* moral universe is shown in the fact that Veronica, though she manages to escape J.D.'s almost hypnotic power over her, nevertheless shares the guilt of his crimes. And the film doesn't try to explain away J.D.'s warped, violent impulses as being rooted in his testosterone levels, but in his profoundly damaged history. We learn that his mother committed suicide by walking into a building moments before his father, a demolition contractor, blew it up. (J.D.'s name gives a clue to his, and the movie's, lineage: he's a spiritual son of tortured fifties' rebel James Dean.) Heathers is a bleakly funny satire of teen movies that nevertheless explores the roots of adolescent angst with a ruthless honesty. Like so many contemporary black comedies, there is a deep well of despair coursing under Heathers, the despair of an entire generation with no one to guide them into adulthood.

One of the aspects of teen movies that many adults dislike is the way they see themselves portrayed in these films. Going back to the days of *Beach Blanket Bingo*, adults are routinely depicted as ridiculous, ineffectual and not too bright. In these older films, there is usually at least one caring, understanding grown-up who intervenes to help solve the kids' problems, but even that convention is disappearing in contemporary pop culture. Nowadays the adult characters in *The Simpsons* and other popular shows are increasingly portrayed as complete and utter buffoons, with nothing to offer their children because they've never grown up themselves. In contemporary teen movies like *Heathers* and *Buffy*, the adults not only don't help solve kids' problems, they actively make things worse. The kids are on their own and they know it. In *Heathers*, this total flight from adult responsibility is mirrored in much of the joking banter between parents and offspring. J.D. calls his father "son" and his father calls him "Dad." Veronica's standard reply to her father's rhetorical inquiries ("Why do I read these spy novels?") is "Because you're an idiot." The real joke is that she believes it's true. Not a single one of the adults in this movie can be counted on to exhibit anything resembling true maturity. Even the caring, feel-good teacher who encourages the students to express their feelings about the wave of suicides ends up engineering the whole experience into a media event, with herself as the star. This adult abdication only accentuates Veronica's utter aloneness in carrying out her heroic task: while her friends cheer on the basketball team in the school gym, she's down in the boiler room stalking J.D. with a gun she barely knows how to use. But she has to rely on herself, because there is absolutely no one else she can go to for help. In the end she risks everything to expose the phony, venal, abusive relationships, the "Antarctica of the soul" she sees everywhere around her, and manages to come out on top. "There's a new sheriff in town," she announces at the end of the film.

Veronica, Buffy and Valerie are all, in their quirky ways, daughters of *Oz*. Like Dorothy they are carving out new paths for female heroes, venturing into new and still largely uncharted territory. So it's very satisfying and not at all surprising that all three films contain explicit homages to *The Wizard of Oz*. Veronica refers to one of the Heathers as "the Wicked Witch of the West — or is it East?" One of the vampires echoes the Witch's famous line when he hisses at Buffy, "I'll get you, and your little dog, too!" (Even though Buffy has no dog.) And Valerie gives a delicious twist to Dorothy's parting line to the Scarecrow, when she bids one of the aliens goodbye: "Wiploc, I think I'll miss you least of all." But at the same time as these new stories about women and girls are in the ascendacy, concerns about the destructive effects of pop culture are becoming stronger than ever, as we'll see in the next chapter.

CHAPTER SIX

Kids, TV Violence and Moral Panic

TELEVISION'S EFFECTS on children have been a focus of concern since the medium's earliest days, and the current outcry about TV violence is nothing new. Back in the fifties and early sixties, programs like *Dragnet* and *The Untouchables* were criticized for allegedly encouraging teenage delinquency. In the seventies, parent groups began to focus on children's television programs themselves, but most of their efforts were directed at the extreme commercialization of these programs, especially the aggressive marketing of toys. Activists like Peggy Charren, founder of Action for Children's Television in the United States, were outraged by the free rein given to toy manufacturers to exploit kids' impressionability with hard-sell ads and endless marketing tie-ins. Charren's group successfully lobbied the FCC for limits on the amount of advertising time allowed during children's programs, but even these modest gains were overturned during the deregulation mania of the Reagan years. Now, in the nineties, the battle over children's TV has moved to a new front, as activists shift their focus from advertising to the content of children's programs.

Events in society at large have had much to do with bringing about this shift. In Canada, the campaign against media violence has been fueled by the terrible event that has come to be known as the Montreal Massacre. In 1991 Pacijou, a Montreal-based anti-violence group, sponsored the creation of an outdoor sculpture consisting of more than 12,000 toy guns, GI Joe figures and other weapons collected from schoolchildren. The sculpture was unveiled on the second anniversary of Marc Lépine's murder of 14 female engineering students at the Ecole Polytechnique in Montreal. The clear implication was that his actions and those of other mass murderers are a direct result of playing with war toys and exposure to violence in the media. Journalist André Picard echoed this sentiment in a *Globe and Mail* column: "Marc Lépine was in many ways a typical boy. He played at war while his sister played at dolls." Another group, the Coalition against Violence in Children's Programming, made the point that war toys and TV violence encourage boys to "play war, a real or imaginary war that will carry over to the home, the classroom and the neighbourhood."

More recently, Virginie Larivière, a Quebec teenager whose sister was sexually assaulted and murdered in 1992, garnered nationwide publicity and the backing of then-Prime Minister Brian Mulroney for gathering over a million signatures on a petition against TV violence. Her efforts led directly to the adoption in early 1994 of a new broadcasters' code aimed at eliminating depictions of "glamorized, gratuitous" violence in children's programs. In the United States, Senator Paul Simon has led a similar crusade against TV violence, and Attorney General Janet Reno has threatened the movie and television industries with anti-violence legislation unless they clean up their act voluntarily. Lately everyone from cable TV magnate Ted Turner to Anwar Sadat's widow Jehane Sadat has jumped on the bandwagon, condemning violence in television and movies and pointing the finger at popular culture as the cause of moral breakdown in society.

No sensible person would argue with the view that there's

too much violence in popular culture. But solutions to the problem are turning out to be more complex than many anti-violence campaigners care to admit. As with the pornography debate, people have widely varying definitions of just what constitutes a violent act or image. By the prevailing method of tallying up violent acts per hour, for example, *Thea,* a sitcom about a black single mother, recently found itself listed among the top ten most violent shows on U.S. television. According to the National Coalition on Television Violence, which compiled the list, acts like grabbing, shoulder tapping and even Thea's threat to "teach her kids a lesson" all qualified as violent acts. This highlights another problem with the approach adopted by anti-violence crusaders, who make no attempt to deal with narrative context or to distinguish between different styles or genres — between comedy and drama, between cartoon and live-action programs.

The anti-violence movement has drawn broad support across the political spectrum, which isn't surprising since no one on the left or the right wants to be regarded as cavalier about violence or, worse, as promoting it. But dissenting voices are starting to surface. Some media critics, noting the large number of politicians on both sides of the border who are hopping onto the anti-violence bandwagon, detect more than a whiff of political opportunism. *Globe and Mail* TV critic Liam Lacey wondered in 1993: "Is the current emotional, anti-violence campaign really about the dangers of television violence, or is it about finding a political scapegoat?" And more recently even Todd Gitlin, a longtime critic of movie and TV violence, took strong issue with the anti-violence crusaders, charging that the movement "distracts attention from the real causes of — and the serious remedies for — the epidemic of violence" in society. Comments like those of anti-violence activist Terry Rakolta of Americans for Responsible Television lend weight to Gitlin's analysis. "We can't seem to fix education, we can't seem to control drugs, but we can take a look at television violence," Rakolta said in a 1994 Canadian current affairs show. In other words, it's far easier to point the finger at television, movies and video games than to look at the complex social roots of violence or to examine the numerous ways we adults have failed our children.

But TV violence is as much a reflection of our current social malaise as it is a cause, and there's a legitimate argument that in focusing on the media, what we're really doing is shooting the messenger rather than genuinely trying to come to grips with the problem. People in the entertainment industry are also concerned that the violence issue is being used to take the edge off hard-hitting shows. Barbara Hall, producer of the series *I'll Fly Away*, said on the same program that U.S. network officials demanded that a scene be cut from one show that depicted a violent Ku Klux Klan attack on blacks. She noted that a writer on another series was recently directed to take out not only violent scenes but ones that "made the system look bad."

The problem is compounded by our own confusion and ambivalence. I once heard a parent say she was worried about what her kids' passion for *The Simpsons* was doing to them, then admit in the next breath that she let them watch *Twin Peaks*. In a magazine profile of Hollywood actor John Malkovich, he expresses concern about the effects of TV and movie violence on his children, then declares that he approves of spanking as a method of discipline and apparently sees no contradiction between the two. As media critic Bronwyn Drainie points out:

> We're all a bit hypocritical about the question of TV violence. Wouldn't you prefer to see Elmer Fudd fill Bugs full of holes than put up with the gagging sweetness of the Care Bears? Isn't the rock video edginess of *Miami Vice* more compelling, and ultimately less offensive, than the bottomless inanity of *Three's Company*? Our own ambivalence about the entertainment value of violence, especially fun violence like cartoons or Hulk Hogan, may keep these disturbing issues permanently unresolved.

This ambivalence is part and parcel of the extraordinary love-hate relationship we have with pop culture, and television in particular. Almost everyone denigrates television, but almost everyone watches it. We speak of the "boob tube" and the "idiot box." TV-bashing is a virtual requirement for anyone who wishes to be considered a literate, cultured person. Rarely before in history has a society so thoroughly disowned an object of its own creation, one that forms such an important part of its very cultural fabric. But to understand the roots of this alarmism about popular culture and the anti-violence fervour it has spawned, we need to put this phenomenon in its historical context.

MORAL PANICS

Waves of moral panic about children's culture have recurred with great regularity and in different guises through the past hundred years. The dime novels of the nineteenth century, as well as the series books of the early twentieth like the *Bobbsey Twins* and *Hardy Boys*, were denounced by educators and child experts in much the same kind of alarmist tones as TV and video games are today. Harmless as they seem to us nowadays, at the time critics charged that these books undermined literacy, encouraged children to challenge authority, confused fantasy with reality and were just plain "trash." In the 1920s, the target shifted to the new visual medium of the silent motion picture, with adults sounding the alarm about the dire effects on the young of all those hours in darkened theatres. In the thirties and forties, experts began to warn about the harmful effects of radio on children. As with television today, studies were published showing that listening to radio was negatively affecting children's behaviour and impairing their ability to distinguish fantasy from reality.

In the fifties, comic books, along with Elvis and rock music, became the great threat. In 1954 psychiatrist Frederic Wertham published *Seduction of the Innocent,* which blamed comics for juvenile delinquency and cited numerous cases of crimes committed by children and teenagers after reading comics. Then, as now, politicians siezed on the issue: the U.S. Congress established a special committee and conducted hearings to explore the alleged link between comics and juvenile crime. This campaign to clean up the comics resulted in the adoption of the Comics Code, which placed severe restrictions on the stories and imagery depicted in comic books. Interestingly, while the Comics Code had the immediate effect of driving some horror and crime comics out of business, its long-term impact has been negligible. The comics of today are as untrammeled as they ever were, but aside from the odd Christian fundamentalist rumblings, few objections are raised about them. In the nineties, TV , movies and video games have taken over to become the targets of the latest wave of moral panic.

It may appear to contemporary crusaders that violence in the popular media is a threat of an entirely different order than these quaint artifacts of the past. But in their day the Rover Boys, silent movies and *True Crime* comics were believed to be every bit as threatening to the existing social order as Ninja Turtles and Terminator movies are today. And the striking similarities in the language used by these moral crusaders of different eras, the similar claims made again and again about the damaging effects on children and on society as a whole, suggest that the problem of pop culture violence is not a thing apart. The current anti-violence crusade actually reflects a much larger well of concern about children's psyches that underlies all these various crusades.

They certainly share some basic assumptions, chief among them being that any endeavour children engage in should serve some higher moral purpose — should, in a word, be educational. This is a burden placed on children's play as well as all their forms of entertainment and is a bias every bit as strong today as it was in the nineteenth century, when children's books were expected to give moral guidance and "build character." Today, of course, we use a different terminology. We speak of "positive role models" and "quality" (meaning educational) programming. But the underlying sentiment is basically the same. Kids' programs without any obvious educational intent are automatically considered junk and garbage, while "quality" children's programs are supposed to be tasteful, not loud or brash — rather like a well-behaved child. But adults and kids tend to have quite different ways of defining quality. Adults routinely distinguish between what's "good" and what they like, between art and mere entertainment. This kind of distinction is quite foreign to most kids. If they like something, they'll tell you it's good. I'll have more to say on this whole question of quality when I look at Saturday morning children's TV in the next chapter.

There's a further irony in the fact that the line between so-called quality programs and commercial children's TV is becoming more blurred all the time. One show that made its mark on educational TV, *Where in the World Is Carmen Sandiego?*, recently jumped from PBS to the highly commercial, lowest-common-denominator Fox Network. *Sesame Street* has successfully straddled the boundary for a long time, packaging its educational content in an unabashedly pop-cult mix of rock music and TV parodies like "Monsterpiece Theater." More recent is the unprecedented commercial success of another PBS show, *Barney and Friends*. Barney's lumbering purple persona currently graces everything from lunchboxes to video compilations of "Barney's Favorites." Early in 1993, some PBS affiliates were roundly criticized for using Barney giveaways as incentives in their annual fundraising drives. Many parents claimed this smacked of the same exploitive tactics that so-called commercial TV had been using on children for years. Things came full circle as Action for Children's Television head Peggy Charren found herself staring down her old enemy, commercialization, on public television of all places. Charren said she found it "extraordinarily inappropriate for PBS to use children to fund-raise."

It's interesting that we adults don't put this burden of being educational on our own entertainment. We acknowledge that we have a range of tastes, moods and interests. We accept that we often turn to so-called "low" culture to feed our desires of the moment. But we're leery of allowing children the same kind of latitude. Partly this comes from an honest, if only half-understood admission that many of these "low" pop culture forms express anti-authoritarian impulses of one sort or another. Dime novels, comics and *The Simpsons* are each in their own way an outlet for kids' natural rebelliousness. So it's not surprising that many adults, and particularly so-called "family values" conservatives, find these things so threatening. They're not wrong: a good deal of pop culture is subversive. It does challenge adult authority over children. But its subversiveness goes even deeper than that. In a society that sees itself as rational, scientific and ruled by self-control, pop culture is the repository of pleasure, of the forbidden, of gratification and freedom from inhibition. It serves, in a sense, as the underside, the id of the larger culture, the place where our more "primitive" impulses and unenlightened behaviours are consigned. Another way to characterize the pop culture battleground is as a struggle between the edu-experts, who know what's good for children, and pop culture purveyors, who have their finger on the pulse of kids' desires. In the words of the Bob Dylan song, they tell kids, "They may know what you need, but I know what you want." An ad for cartoon shows on the Fox Network presents this dichotomy in perfectly distilled form. It opens with Tom (of *Tom and Jerry*) slamming the door on an unmistakable caricature of PBS's avuncular Mr. Rogers and exhorts kids not to waste time on such boring fare but to "tune in to where the action is."

History gives us good reason to be wary of these waves of

moral panic, since they've often led to wholesale and sometimes bizarre efforts to censor children's culture. We're seeing this now in the odd alliance of left and right to control the content of children's literature. What binds them is a long-standing suspicion of fantasy and a belief that children's exposure to ideas, stories and images should be strictly controlled. So while feminists are upset about sex-stereotyping in traditional fairy tales and anti-violence parents are appalled at a character's threat to "pound God into applesauce" in Robert Munsch's *Giant*, right-wing fundamentalists in the United States and Canada are carrying on a campaign to get a highly regarded reading anthology series, *Impressions*, banned in schools because they find its fairy tales and fantasy stories rife with Satanism and New Age content. And in Long Island, N.Y., a parent even managed to have copies of the popular *Where's Waldo?* books removed from her local library after she spotted a partially exposed woman's breast in one of the book's dense illustrations.

MONKEY SEE, MONKEY DO?

"Children believe what they see on TV. Children want to be what they see on TV. Children become what they see on TV." This quote by Dr. Arlette Lefebvre, a psychiatrist, at Toronto's Hospital for Sick Children, succinctly sums up a belief that has become an article of faith in the anti-violence movement, as well as an underlying assumption of earlier moral crusades. According to this view, popular culture is essentially a monkey-see, monkey-do proposition: violent behaviour is simply a learned response to stories and imagery that depict violence. It therefore follows that the way to reduce or eliminate violence in society is to reduce or eliminate those stories and images. As Virginie Larivière rather wistfully put it when she presented her petition to the Canadian public: "If all the violence and death stops on TV, maybe it will stop in real life."

Unfortunately, real life is not so simple or easily controlled. Although a considerable body of research suggests that there is a relationship between violence on TV and children's behaviour, it's far from clear that this relationship is a simple cause-and-effect one. Dorothy and Jerome Singer, who survey the available research in their 1990 book *The House of Make-Believe*, suggest that a complex of interrelated factors influences children's behaviour, including the overall family "culture" they are raised in, the amount of TV they are exposed to and how well-developed their imaginative lives are. In their own studies, the Singers found that certain factors tended to form clusters; for example, families with a more authoritarian style of communication, who tended to use physical punishment, also tended to have heavy TV-viewing habits. As well, children in these families tended to have a less-developed ability to fantasize or engage in imaginative play. The higher levels of aggressive behaviour found in such children are more properly seen as stemming from this cluster of factors rather than any one of them. These studies by the Singers and others suggest while TV viewing is an important factor, it is only one of several implicated in stimulating violent behaviour.

But television, movies and video games provide such obvious, readily available targets that they have come to be seen, in the minds of many people, as the cause of violence in real life. More and more the idea that TV causes violence is taken at face value, as something so obvious to anyone with an ounce of common sense that it doesn't require proof. This is akin to the stance taken by anti-porn activists, who are faced with a similar lack of conclusiveness in the research on the effects of pornography. But a critical point continually glossed over by anti-violence and anti-porn crusaders bears repeating: Stating the common-sense fact that there is a relationship between media violence and real-life violence, between male consumption of pornography and violence against women, is not the same as saying media violence and pornography cause violent behaviour. Unless this relationship is understood in all its complexity, censorship-type solutions, for all that they appear quick and easy, will fail to yield the resulting behavioural and societal changes. Furthermore, as we've seen time and again, these types of measures too often backfire, resulting in wide-scale suppression of all kinds of imagery and ideas that may have less to do with violence than with challenging the status quo.

The campaign against TV violence in Colombia illustrates just how attractive, and how wrong-headed, this approach can be. In the spring of 1993, a Bogotá mother made headlines when she complained that her sons were "beating up on their little sister" because of the violence they were watching on television. Daisy Porto de Vargas managed to get a court injunction against several programs and in the process ushered in a wave of protest and government measures, including a censor board that cut what it considered violent scenes from a host of TV programs, including *The Simpsons*. In a country where the homicide rate is eight times that of the United States,' these measures may have seemed not only appropriate but long overdue. But critics of the measures pointed out that Colombia's high rate of violent crime long predated the widespread introduction of television. Politically motivated violence and power struggles between rival drug cartels have far more to do with violence in Colombian society than pop culture. And predictably, many of the programs that came under the censor board's knife were soap operas, targeted more for graphic sex than for violent content.

Increasingly, a more sophisticated theory of "desensitization" has gained currency among critics of TV violence. The idea here is that children gradually become desensitized to real-life violence because of the large number of shootings and murders they witness on TV, and this in turn makes them more likely to condone violent acts and engage in them themselves. Some media experts, like the University of Toronto's Johnathon Freedman, have serious reservations about the desensitization theory. Freedman claims that children do indeed become desensitized, but only to TV violence itself, which they know to be fake. Their abhorrence of real-life violence, he maintains, remains undiminished.

The case of two teenagers who held up and murdered a man in a Burlington, Ontario, gas station would appear to lend some credence to the desensitization theory. Steven Olah and James Ruston were two deeply disturbed youths whose predisposition to violent fantasies and aggressive behaviour had surfaced numerous times before the "thrill murder" they carried out in the fall of 1989. Given their histories, it's difficult to believe that their ample exposure to pop culture violence alone led them to kill an unsuspecting customer at the gas bar where Ruston worked. But clearly movies and TV had distorted their perceptions of violence, and this apparently had a bearing on how they carried out the crime. According to Ruston, their intention wasn't to kill the victim, but only to knock him unconscious so they could steal his wallet and credit cards. They panicked when they discovered that knocking a person out is much harder than it looks in the movies. "We never counted on it taking like 10 bonks to knock the guy out," Olah told police. "We've seen it in the movies all the time; you hit him once and down he goes."

But Ruston and Olah also clearly fit the prototype of the "low-fantasy" children studied by Dorothy and Jerome Singer. Such children, they found, had a diminished capacity to process and integrate the violent imagery they were exposed to and were more likely than highly imaginative children to engage in actual aggressive behaviour. Other researchers, such as James Gilligan of the Massachusetts Center for the Study of Violence, are finding that impairment of the ability to fantasize lies at the root of much violent behaviour. "The difference between a real rapist and a rape fantasy is that the real rapist hasn't learned the difference between fantasy and reality," Gilligan argues. "The person who knows how to play is the person least likely to [commit violence] in real life." This helps to explain why the majority of children who watch violent programs don't act out what they see. It may well be that the ones who grow up to be wife beaters and serial killers are the ones who never learned how to play, whose ability to use fantasy to process and integrate the images and experiences they are exposed to has been deeply, irreparably damaged.

It may be that we're not asking the right question. Maybe what we should be looking at is not "Does watching TV cause violence?" but "Does watching TV harm the imagination?" The Singers express strong concerns about television's impact on kids' ability to play and to fantasize, and they cite a considerable body of evidence suggesting it diminishes rather than enhances the development of the imagination. But their work also points to the amount of viewing time, rather than simple exposure to television, as the critical factor. "Heavy" viewers who watched more than about 25 hours of television a week showed marked impairment of their imaginative capabilities, while children who watched little or moderate amounts of TV did not. It makes sense that heavy viewing takes away from imaginative play. We know that a child's imaginative capacities are chiefly developed through play, and children who spend the bulk of their waking hours watching TV literally have less time to play. Also, children need enough tube-free time to process the imagery and stories they see on TV and use them in their play. Otherwise they can become swamped and overloaded. Prolonged TV watching also has a mesmerizing, almost numbing effect that can leave kids with little time and energy for more active life experiences. As anthropologist Ashley Montagu has observed, the danger of TV is that we end up "watching life instead of living it." But overall, the research on TV and imagination suggests that the content of what children watch may be a less important factor in shaping them than the amount of TV they watch. This critical point is one that the anti-violence crusaders have largely overlooked in their zeal to eliminate violent content from children's programming.

CARTOONS AND CONTEXT

Another area of controversy in the TV violence debate centres on reality and fantasy, and children's ability to distinguish between the two. Kids don't understand that much of the violence they see on TV is fiction, not "real," the argument goes, and so they must be shielded from it. But the whole question of children's ability to distinguish reality from fantasy is meaningless without some reference to age. Everything we know about cognitive development indicates that there is a huge gulf between a two-year-old and a seven-year-old in this regard. In fact, coming to an understanding of the concept of fantasy and learning to use it in imaginative play is a large part of what early childhood is all about. What folk wisdom calls the age of reason, around seven years, actually has less to do with logic than with a child's ability to use abstract concepts, to understand "what-if" narratives as opposed to the more literal, concrete thought processes of the two-year-old. To the latter child, everything she sees, on TV or anywhere else, is "real" to her, because she doesn't know yet that any distinction exists between these two modes, reality and fantasy, fact and fiction. This understanding is one, however, that she will gradually develop over the next several years. Some child development experts are concerned that television and other forms of pop culture are doing damage to the natural development of this ability. They argue that TV's seductiveness and its all-pervasive influence are swamping kids' ability to tell what's real and what's not. The Singers cite studies showing that even 10- and 11-year-olds had trouble separating actors' real-life identities from the characters they portrayed on television.

But there's little in the way of conclusive research in this area. And a key problem in the whole discussion is that not enough effort is made to distinguish between television's different modalities. The medium exposes children as well as adults to images of violence in three distinctly different contexts: "real" or documentary violence on news and current events programs; fictional, live-action violence on cop shows, Westerns and other action dramas; and animated cartoons, which are characterized by their lack of realism in depicting violence, as well as everything else. The lines between these categories, especially between the first two, are becoming more blurred by the popularity of such shows as *Rescue-911* and tabloid TV programs like *A Current Affair,* which present actual news footage in highly dramatized formats. Still, our knowledge of perceptual processes suggests to us that these modalities are not taken in by the brain in the same way. Media watchdog groups routinely ignore violence on the news while lumping the other two categories together in their violent-acts-per-hour tallies. Yet some experts speculate that watching real-life violence on the news is more harmful to children, because they know full well that it's not fake, that real people have been hurt or killed.

With cartoons, the situation becomes even more complicated. Even very young children, who may not yet be able to distinguish "reality" on the news from sitcom "fantasy," are well aware that what they are watching in cartoons is a picture, akin to a drawing they might make themselves, rather than a literal depiction of reality. Yet cartoons, because their audience is mainly children and because their slam-bang style presents such a highly visible target, have become a major focus of the anti-violence crusade. Cartoon shows consistently come out high in the violent-acts-per-hour yardstick surveys, and one Canadian study released in the summer of 1994 found them to have "the highest level of violence of all TV programs." Shows like *Teenage Mutant Ninja Turtles* are regularly cited by anti-violence groups as averaging over a hundred violent acts per hour, which appears to make them far more violent than, say, prime-time cop shows. But we should question whether it's really accurate to use the same word "violence" to describe what goes on in both cartoons and live-action shows. Is a drug dealer shooting a cop on *NYPD Blue* the equivalent of Yosemite Sam shooting Bugs Bunny? Although there's been little if any specific research in this area, our knowledge of cognitive processes suggests that the brain takes in the two images quite differently. Cartoons, after all, don't even attempt to create the illusion of reality that live-action movies and TV shows do. By their very nature they are patently unreal, featuring characters that in no way resemble live persons and routinely depicting events that are physically impossible in real life. In one sense, this is the exhilarating freedom of animation, both for the animator and the viewer. A falling anvil flattens a character into a pancake; instantly she pops back into shape like an accordion. A cannon shoots another character into the stratosphere; a few frames later he's sauntering along, whistling.

But it's this very aspect of animation that causes some experts like George Gerbner of the highly regarded Annenberg School for Communications at the University of Pennsylvania to argue that cartoon violence is actually more pernicious than live-action because it is "violence without consequences." Gerbner calls it "happy violence; it all has a happy ending" and claims it gives children a distorted picture of the real-life consequences of violence. Gerbner's views were cited in media reports about an Ohio boy who set fire to his own home in 1993, killing his younger sister. The boy was allegedly inspired by the firesetting activities of notorious MTV cartoon characters Beavis and Butt-head.

But a somewhat curious double standard seems to be taking hold among some critics of cartoon violence. While contemporary cartoons like *Ninja Turtles* and *Stunt Dawgs* come under heavy criticism for violence, the same acts are excused as "extreme pratfall humour" when they appear in classic cartoons like Warner Brothers' *Bugs Bunny*. There were media reports that *Bugs Bunny* and *Roadrunner* would be exempted from the new Canadian broadcasters' TV violence code, despite the frequency with which they use things like guns and dynamite, because CRTC chairman Keith Spicer felt they were harmless and had a personal fondness for them. This is another example of the nostalgia I discussed in Chapter Two, and how it colours adults' responses to childhood and pop culture.

It's certainly true that slapstick violence and animation have gone hand-in-hand since the form was invented. *Itchy and Scratchy*, the scathingly funny cartoon-within-a-cartoon on *The Simpsons,* offers an ongoing compendium of this slam-bang cartoon tradition. Each mini-episode consists of little else than a series of strategems by Itchy (or is it Scratchy?) to maim, blow away or otherwise do grievous harm to Scratchy (or is it Itchy?). Somewhat paradoxically, *Itchy and Scratchy* is also a celebration of animation itself and its freedom to depict the forbidden and impossible, "without consequences," subject only to the limits of the imagination. The irony is that although *Itchy and Scratchy* is clearly meant to satirize mindless cartoon violence, its high violent-acts-per-hour tally would almost assure its demise under most of the proposed anti-violence measures.

POP CULTURE REVISIONISTS

In the face of such overwhelming societal disapproval, it takes almost an act of courage to defend popular culture as being something that's good for children. The entertainment industry, of course, has a vested interest in promoting its products. But even producers of children's entertainment, who in some ways have their finger on the pulse of Kid Culture better than any of us, tend to justify what they do as merely "harmless entertainment," not as a positive social good. But true enthu-siasts for popular culture do exist and can be found mostly in universities. A whole new generation of academics, most born in the baby boom era or later, are taking pop culture seriously and studying it with the same passionate, footnoted thor-oughness that their predecessors devoted to more "serious" subjects. This new generation of pop culture theorists has been heavily influenced by modern semiotics and the ideas of European deconstructionist thinkers like Julia Kristeva and Umberto Eco, a fact that shows up in their often dense, jar-gon-ridden prose styles. Probably the best known of them, and easily the most notorious, is Camille Paglia, who became a darling of the media in the early nineties making talk-show appearances where she spoke of *Charlie's Angels* and Aristotle in the same breath. But in many ways Paglia, with her all-over-the-map but ultimately quite conservative politics, is atypical of pop culture theorists, most of whom tend to situ-ate themselves on the left end of the political spectrum. And though they share many of the same concerns about racism, sexism and violence that motivate pop culture's fiercest critics, these younger academics reject what they see as a simplistic, one-dimensional analysis. In their view, the purveyors of moral panic don't really understand popular culture or how it works. In particular, they don't understand that global mass culture is a fundamentally new, quasi-evolutionary phenome-non that is itself an outgrowth of the technological revolution.

Marsha Kinder is one of the few pop culture academics who has focused specifically on children's entertainment. In her 1991 book *Playing with Power in Movies, Television and Video Games,* Kinder cites extensive research carried out by Patricia Greenfield and others showing that using computers and playing video games have positive effects on children's cognitive development and motor skills. She also looks at the popular media's growing use of postmodernist techniques:

instantaneousness, a fragmented style of presentation and, especially, self-referentiality or, to use the term preferred by Kinder and other semiotics enthusiasts, "intertextuality." This refers to the ubiquitous phenomenon of pop culture artifacts spawning and feeding off other pop culture artifacts. Kinder points to the *Teenage Mutant Ninja Turtle* phenomenon as a prime example, showing how it began life as a comic book that generated a series of successful feature films, a TV cartoon and numerous marketing spinoffs, including toys and other items based on the Turtle characters. Kinder finds Kid Culture particularly rife with such examples of intertextuality, showing how contemporary cartoons typically draw on other media forms and genres for storylines. She analyzes an episode of *Garfield* in which the couch-potato cat gets trapped inside his own TV , where he's forced to play out various roles such as a character in a Western and a game-show contestant, before managing to escape back into "normal" life.

Kinder argues that pop culture is helping to foster media literacy and to prepare our children to function effectively in a fragmented, technology-dominated postmodern world. But she sees this coming with a high price. For while the intertextual nature of pop culture helps, as she says, "to facilitate cognitive development, yet at the same time it associates this developmental progress with consumerism (a connection the child retains in later life), thereby enabling our consumerist culture to acquire the child functionally." Kinder is leery not only of consumerism but also of what she sees as pervasive sexism in popular culture. Along with Patricia Greenfield, she is concerned about the sex-stereotyped plot lines of typical video games. And the fact that video games are far more popular with boys than girls means that it is boys who will reap the cognitive benefits documented by Greenfield's research and thus acquire the computer-age skills they need to succeed.

Kinder views pop culture with considerable ambivalence. But John Fiske's take on the subject is decidedly more positive. In his books *Understanding Popular Culture* and *Reading the Popular*, Fiske ranges over the whole spectrum of mass culture. Though he doesn't give particular focus to Kid Culture itself, when I first encountered his work I was struck by how well his approach fit with my own observations about how kids interact with pop culture. Fiske agrees with Kinder and other leftist critics that pop culture conveys a host of socially retrograde messages including consumerism, male domination and the inherent superiority of white Western cultures. But he emphatically rejects what he sees as these critics' determinist perspective: the widespread, largely unquestioned belief that popular culture is, to paraphrase Marx's famous dictum about religion, the "opiate of the people," the mechanism by which the power structure controls the lives, desires and even the thoughts of ordinary people. By putting all the emphasis on the texts or messages, Fiske argues, we are missing the other equally important side of the equation: how people take in or "read" the texts and messages. In Fiske's view, the public is not made up of the passive, couch-potato consumers of pop culture fodder commonly dismissed and reviled by the literate middle class. The system or the power structure may create the products, he argues, but it cannot control how people will use them or what meaning they will assign to them. People create their own meaning out of pop culture; in his terminology, they are "active readers" and even "producers." One striking example of what Fiske calls a "producerly" text is the *Star Trek* phenomenon. Ever since the original TV series went into perpetual reruns in response to audience pressure, fans have claimed the various incarnations of *Star Trek* as their own. Trekkers, as they prefer to be called, not only exert a strong influence on the phenomenon's evolution, they are actively involved in creating it — learning and speaking Klingon, the show's made-up language, for instance, or adopting an alien alter ego complete with name and costume. That Trek fans have become actual co-creators is a fact frequently acknowledged by the show's producers.

But audiences aren't content simply to make their own meanings. According to Fiske, they also use the tools of pop culture — the images, stories and consumer goods — to challenge and subvert the very power structure that produced them. Just as a capitalist will sell you the rope to hang him with, as Lenin reportedly once remarked, people use the oppressor's tools to carry out a kind of guerrilla resistance against the dominant culture. In doing so, they try to create spaces where they can be in control, where they can resist domination and maintain their own sense of identity. This resistance is not the same as open opposition, because by and large it takes place not in the political arena, but in the realm of everyday life. This is what Fiske calls the "art of making do," and it is not a simple or straightforward process to pin down. Fiske treats pop culture as the fluid, inherently paradoxical, quintessentially modern phenomenon that it is, and to suggest the contradictory nature of these resistance efforts he more than once invokes the image of the Trickster archetype from various native traditions.

Fiske is not only critical of intellectuals who dismiss popular culture as "low" and "vulgar"; he also has a problem with the typical left-wing view that it is an overpoweringly manipulative force in contemporary life. In his view, both stances betray a fundamental misunderstanding of pop culture's powerful appeal. He takes leftists and feminists to task for their wet-blanket approach. They have, in his estimation, "failed to produce a positive theory of popular pleasure. The result of this is that their theories can all too easily appear puritanical; the society they envision is not one in which fun plays much part, if it exists at all ...." For Fiske, popular culture is largely about fun, pleasure and fulfilling desires; he calls it "the carnival of the body" and argues that Western culture's terror of the body and of pleasure goes a long way towards explaining why popular entertainments have always been seen as corrupting and dangerous. He explores the way in which pop culture's pervasive consumerism can also be seen as a validation of desire. For all that pop culture warps our desires and creates longings it cannot fulfil, its message that pleasure is not bad but good and its promise that we can have what we want are profoundly radical in a dysfunctional, pleasure-phobic culture like ours. In my view, part of kids' powerful attraction to pop culture stems from the fact that they naturally gravitate to the positive, to what will give them pleasure. Adults think there's something wrong with this, that children's natural desires are dangerous and need to be controlled. Desire, then, is the battleground on which a large part of the war between children and adults over popular culture is being waged.

I find Fiske's perspective offers a bracing antidote to the common view of children as passive vessels, as robots whose minds and hearts are completely in thrall to the demons of Saturday morning TV. Like adults, children make their own meanings out of the raw material of popular culture. In fact, Fiske cites research suggesting that children may be more adept at reading pop culture messages than adults are. Throughout this book I've tried to present examples of kids' multileveled responses to pop culture and the way in which they, in Fiske's words, "turn cultural commodities to their own interests and find pleasure in using them to make their own meanings." In the next chapter, I'll give some examples of what he calls "open" texts in Kid Culture, ones that leave room for interpretations that are different from, sometimes even contradictory to, what they appear to be on the surface.

CHAPTER SEVEN

Re-Viewing Saturday Morning

"SATURDAY MORNING HELL," the title of a 1993 *Globe and Mail* feature article on children's television, put into words the way a lot of parents feel. By her own account, journalist Alanna Mitchell spent a month of Saturday mornings watching popular cartoons like *Teenage Mutant Ninja Turtles* and *Dog City*, and her descriptions of what she saw run the gamut from "disturbing" to "vile" to "gruesome." (Her three-year-old daughter was banished to another room during the exercise.) The term "Saturday Morning," in fact, refers less to a specific time (most of the shows also run in after-school time slots) than to an entire category that, to Mitchell and many other adults, represents all that is most repellent about children's television. They see these shows as pure, unadulterated junk — crassly commercial, saturated with sexism and violence, totally lacking any redeeming social or educational value. The cartoons, in particular, are the kind of high-decibel, frantically paced shows that make adults want to scream, "How can you watch that garbage?"

Most of us are familiar with these shows only as a barrage of irritating background noise. Not many adults do what Mitchell did and actually sit down and watch any of them. But garbage, like beauty, is in the eye of the beholder, and to the young audiences they are aimed at, these shows are anything but garbage — they are funny, exciting, entertaining.

Certainly some Saturday morning shows are better than others, a fact that kids who watch them freely acknowledge. But as I've argued elsewhere in this book, there is a real gap between adult and childhood sensibilities. The "problem" of Saturday morning television has as much to do with adults' expectations and perceptions as with the programs themselves. Typical Saturday morning shows, like so much children's entertainment, are done in a kind of pumped-up, low-comedy style that appeals to kids but tends to turn off adults, especially middle-class, educated adults. If they are able to overcome that "taste gap" and watch with a more open mind, adults might be surprised by the interesting social content and overtly political dimensions of some Saturday morning shows. Though they rarely attempt to be "educational" in a didactic way, many of these "junk-food" shows do explore pressing social issues and reflect kids' own world back to them with a greater honesty than many so-called quality programs. Adults claim that children have no taste, that they can't discriminate between what's junk and what's worthwhile. But in the case of Saturday morning television, I would suggest that it's adults who have the problem distinguishing between good and bad, between quality and junk, because they have no feel for the genres and don't know how to "read" them.

One thing that often mystifies me about adults is our tendency to almost willfully dismiss any signs of positive change in kids' culture. It's almost as if we have an investment in believing that things are as bad as ever, if not worse. Mitchell, for example, finds Saturday morning cartoons "rampant" with "extreme sexism .... It's as if the social gains women have made over the past generation have been wiped out with the stroke of a cartoonist's pen." She quotes another researcher's claim that "since 1983, we've seen a real resurgence of sex-role stereotyping. It's a terrible regression." But I find it patently untrue, as a surprising number of feminists continue to argue, that the women's movement has had virtually no impact on the popular media. Feminism has been quietly seeping into popular culture over the past decade, and, as I'll show in this chapter, Saturday morning kids' TV is no exception. But it's a wilder, woollier, often politically incorrect brand of feminism that some of the more sober minded activists may not readily recognize. In fact, some of the shows adults consider the worst offenders are the ones exploring the most progressive themes, carving out newer, fresher territory than most adult-oriented entertainment.

Along with sexism and violence, the other frequent charge against Saturday morning television is that it's completely commercialized, with the content ruled by advertising considerations. One critic complained that the *Mighty Morphin Power Rangers* series was nothing but "one long toy commercial." According to Toronto media researcher Sandra Campbell, "There's been a complete fusion of television and toys. [These shows] are infomercials, only parents don't know any of this." While I'll admit that the influence of commercial tie-ins on children's shows is enormous and problematic, I don't agree that they are solely what these shows are all about, and I think it's unfair for adults to dismiss the entire genre on that basis. Commerce and popular entertainment have always had strong ties, after all. And the writers and animation artists who toil in the children's TV industry are craftspeople, for whom considerations of "quality" do play a part in their work, whether adults can recognize it or not.

TOUGH GIRLS AND TURTLES

One of the things adults might notice if they begin to watch Saturday morning TV rather than just fulminate against it is the growing presence of female characters in action cartoons. For a long time this genre was almost exclusively male, with the odd female character like Princess Leia of the *Star Wars* trilogy playing the requisite damsel-in-need-of-rescue role. But in the early eighties, along came She-Ra, the first and for a long time the only female to break through the "glass ceiling" of the superhero world. Though she tended to favour skimpy, fairly revealing outfits, She-Ra's body was quite strong and muscular, certainly more normally proportioned than, say, Barbie's. (If Barbie were a real-life woman, it's safe to conclude that she'd eventually wind up in a body cast.) She-Ra hung out with He-Man and other male superheroes, and for a while in the mid-eighties she had her own cartoon show and rang up modest but respectable sales as a doll. (Male superheroes, of course, are never referred to as "dolls" but are marketed as "action figures.") There was no doubt that She-Ra was a full-fledged superhero, though: her full moniker was She-Ra, Princess of Power, and when she raised her magic crystal sword and announced in stentorian tones, "I am She-Ra!" it was clear this was one female who was not to be messed with.

She-Ra has been consigned to the dustbin of out-of-fashion toys, but she was clearly a trailblazer, a woman ahead of her time. In the nineties, female action heroes are finally making their mark in the world of children's entertainment. In fact, since 1992 there's been a quiet revolution going on in Saturday morning television with the appearance of shows such as *X-Men, Cadillacs and Dinosaurs, Where in the World Is Carmen Sandiego?* and *Mighty Morphin Power Rangers,* all of which prominently feature strong female characters who work side by side as equals with male action heroes. These shows fly in the face of the longstanding conventional wisdom that young males won't tolerate females invading their territory. As recently as 1991, network executives were still justifying the almost total lack of female characters on Saturday morning with the insistence that boys had a "deeply ingrained" resistance to female characters and would "refuse to watch" shows that featured them.

It's not surprising that shows like *X-Men* and *Cadillacs and Dinosaurs* would break with conventional wisdom, since they have their roots in the comic book world, where politically adventurous subject matter is common fare. Tough female characters have gradually become a staple of alternative and mainstream comics over the past decade. In late 1993, DC Comics introduced a new comic aimed at teens featuring Anima, "a suicide blonde in Doc Martens and a ripped T-shirt" who battles sexism, racism, homophobia and drugs. Marvel Comics' *X-Men* series has been around for decades and is largely male-dominated. But despite its title, the new animated TV spinoff has something approaching honest-to-goodness gender parity. Of the eight regular mutant characters (named X-Men because they are disciples of the disabled Professor Xavier, who gets around in a kind of hovercraft wheelchair), four are women: Storm, a black woman who can control the weather; Rogue, a deep-south white trash girl who can fly as well as drain power from an opponent; Jean Grey, a telepath; and Jubilee, a teenager who's still learning how to control her inborn mutant powers. The female X-Men do plenty of rescuing as well as being rescued, and though the storylines tend to focus more on the male characters — especially the prickly and pugnacious Wolverine — the women certainly come much closer to getting their fair share of story time than in most kids' shows.

X-Men has other enlightened elements besides strong female characters. Like much contemporary Kid Culture, it revolves around the themes of mutation and metamorphosis. Like the Ninja Turtles and the Power Rangers, the X-Men are a group set apart by their mutant qualities, who can "morph" or transform themselves into super-powerful beings. But *X-Men* uses this theme in an overtly political way. Though they try to use their powers to serve humanity, the X-Men are constantly being attacked and driven underground by right-wing demagogues and other narrow-minded people who denounce them for being different and "abnormal." There are obvious parallels here with racism and gay-bashing. One storyline in the series, in fact, had the X-Men and other mutants being unfairly blamed for the spread of a new, unnamed plague, with unmistakable echoes of AIDS and the spectre of homophobia. Some adults will argue that these themes are too subtle for kids, that they won't get the message unless it's spelled out for them. But this is an objection that any serious writer for young audiences would reject out of hand. Allegory and fable, after all, are time-honoured genres for conveying values and morals to children, as Aesop well knew. In contrast to a show like *GI Joe*, which revels in U.S. jingoism, *X-Men* also has a refreshingly international perspective. One story takes place entirely in Storm's home village in Africa, where she assists at the birth — at home, with a midwife, no less — of her childhood friend's son, to whom she becomes a "second mother." Another episode sends Wolverine back to his ancestral home and native land, which turns out to be Canada. This particular segment featured a collection of true North mutants only a Canadian could fully appreciate: a Sasquatch, two flying francophones and a female who can morph into various forest creatures, among them a snowy owl.

The themes of being different and of the body transforming into something alien clearly have a powerful appeal for the budding pre-adolescents who watch shows like *X-Men.* The character of Jubilee, the teenager, particularly strikes a sympathetic chord with her feelings of being an outcast, her clumsiness and inability to control the changes her body is going through as her mutant powers begin to assert themselves. Her lament "I didn't ask to be a mutant" and her longing to be just a "normal" girl are veritable mirrors of adolescent angst. It's noteworthy that in the *X-Men* universe, as well as on the newer mega-hit *Mighty Morphin Power Rangers,* mutant powers typically emerge in adolescence, a period of life that is viewed in many cultures as a time of initiation and of coming into one's own. The sexual politics of *X-Men* and *Cadillacs and Dinosaurs* also mirror the "buddy" relationships typical of contemporary pre-teens. The male and female characters work as partners and though both shows have them engaging in a fair amount of flirtatious banter, the relationships are mostly platonic. The sexual tensions and attractions are kept largely under the surface, which is where pre-adolescents prefer to keep them.

A typical adult criticism of action cartoons is that they present violence as the solution to all problems and perpetuate a simplistic good-guy/bad-buy view of the world. The amount of physical combat in *X-Men* is typical of the action genre, but what I find interesting about the series is the extent to which it constantly blurs the line between good and evil. A character who is a good guy in one episode can serve as a villain in another, after which he or she is just as likely to revert to being good again. Even the villains are rarely all bad, and most of the continuing characters have a major flaw that frequently drives the storylines. Wolverine, for example, has a raging, uncontrollable temper that often gets him in trouble and puts him at odds with the rest of the X-Men. In the *X-Men* universe, everyone is a mixture of good and bad, and the whole question of good and evil is portrayed with a sophistication that suggests to me that the show's creators are giving young viewers more credit than do many of its critics. If *X-Men* has a single over-riding theme, it is the tolerance for, and even celebration of, diversity. Yet for all that, Alanna Mitchell singled out the show in her *Globe* piece as "grotesquely violent." Along with *Teenage Mutant Ninja Turtles*, *X-Men* became one of the early targets of the new Canadian broadcasters' anti-violence code. Several Canadian stations pulled both series from their Saturday morning schedules as soon as the new code came into effect in early 1994.

NOT-SO-HARD-SHELLED HEROES

Since the late eighties, the Teenage Mutant Ninja Turtles have been the favourite whipping boys for many of our society's ills. Their name is invariably mentioned whenever the links between violence, young boys and TV are raised. When the third *Ninja Turtle* movie proved to be only a modest box-office success in 1993, it was clear that, after half a dozen years, the craze was finally on the wane. But at its height, the Ninja Turtles were blamed for causing playground and day-care fights, including one particularly notorious piece of urban folklore involving a child in a Ninja Turtle costume who pulled a knife on another child during a fight over a toy. (Presumably if the boy hadn't been dressed as a Turtle, the fact that he was carrying a knife would have been dismissed as mere garden-variety playground violence.)

The picture of the Turtles that emerges out of all this, for those who've never watched the TV show or seen the movies (and many of their fiercest critics have not), is of ruthless, macho martial arts practitioners, so I was quite surprised when I got around to checking out the Turtles myself. Could it really be, I wondered, that these rangy, pizza-inhaling pre-pubescents with the high-pitched nasal voices are training our sons to be wife beaters and serial killers?

Granted, *Teenage Mutant Ninja Turtles* is strictly formula entertainment and, in the case of the TV series, not particularly good formula entertainment at that. While I don't want to argue that Ninja Turtles is just "harmless entertainment" (the typical protestation of those in the industry), I do think the real meaning of the phenomenon has been widely misunderstood. Virtually every expert who cites the show presumes it to be endorsing violence, to be saying that, in the words of one critic, "physical aggression as a way of solving problems is O.K." In fact, something considerably more complicated, and more interesting, is going on in the Ninja Turtles' universe.

My own conclusion is that, far from blithely endorsing violence, *Ninja Turtles* is as much about boys' struggle for
impulse control, specifically their struggle not to lash out
indiscriminately, not to see physical retaliation as the solution
to every frustration. Related to this is a theme that has a particular resonance for our times — a boy's search for a truly
loving father. For me, watching the first two Ninja Turtle
movies brought up not disgust at male aggression, but sym-
pathy for young boys' predicament of having to grow up in
the absence of support from caring fathers and older male
mentors.

Much of the misunderstanding surrounding the Turtles
stems from the fact that so many adults know them only
from commercials for Ninja Turtle action figures, which typically make them look meaner and more bellicose than than
they are in their movies and TV show. In the same way, the
ads for *X-Men* and *Star Trek* action figures rarely feature the
female characters, which gives a distorted view of both shows.
Most parents, in fact, have little awareness of the history of
the *Ninja Turtles* phenomenon, which I think is critical to
understanding its appeal. For however much they may look
like a fad fabricated and engineered by toy marketing executives, the Turtles have decidedly more grass-roots origins.
They were created in 1983 by two freelance artists, Kevin
Eastman and Peter Laird, as a send-up of superhero comics,
Marvel Comics' *Daredevil* in particular. Eastman and Laird
produced the first *Ninja Turtle* comic book themselves and
financed it with personal loans and their own savings. The
parodic tone of the early issues helped make it an underground success in the comic book subculture. But as the
Turtles' popularity grew through the mid-eighties, it spilled
over into the mainstream, as more and more young boys
became enamoured of the quirky half-shell heroes and their
martial arts prowess. The Turtles' success is a good example
of the complicated interplay between audience-consumers

and the entertainment industry, and how it continually re-defines and re-creates popular culture. Initially it was the young male audience that embraced and then nurtured the *Ninja Turtle* mythos. Only once it had become a bona fide pop culture phenomenon did Hollywood and the toy compa-nies jump on the bandwagon, and the *Teenage Mutant Ninja Turtle* industry was born.

Contrary to popular belief, marketing techniques can only go so far towards creating these kinds of phenomena. The entertainment industry is forever in search of its Holy Grail, the smash hit, but producers and advertisers freely admit that the process by which this happens is as mysterious to them as anyone else. There's no sure-fire formula for success, and the public can be only be manipulated to a certain extent. The astounding success of the Ninja Turtles was due to more than just savvy marketing. Young boys adopted the Ninja Turtle mythology because (in a way that left adults completely baf-fled) it captured the young male Zeitgeist and spoke to some of their most passionate likes and deep-seated concerns. In a real sense, boys fell in love with Leonardo, Donatello, Michaelangelo and Raphael, and at the height of the craze there were reports of boys going to sleep clutching their heroes like teddy bears, which suggests a more tender bond than the show's critics might have realized. All the Ninja trap-pings are really just window-dressing for the emotional con-nection and identification boys feel with these slimy, oversized amphibians, with their echoes of the enchanted frogs and toads that symbolize emerging sexuality in the animal-groom cycle of fairy tales. This makes sense, because the Turtles are quintessential pre-adolescent males, forever horsing around, constantly eating (or thinking about it) and bashfully frenetic in the presence of grown-up women like April O'Neill.

The character of April, the token female in the *Turtles* saga, has prompted much of the criticism of the show. She's supposedly a smart, gutsy TV news reporter, but she invari-

ably stumblebums her way into trouble and winds up needing to be rescued by the Turtles. Certainly no one can accuse
the show's producers of enlightened sexual politics. But April
does more than simply serve as resident damsel-in-distress.
She's partly a mother-substitute for the orphaned Turtles, but
more importantly, she serves as an embodiment of the adult
female sexuality that both fascinates and terrifies them.

But, typical of the "buddy" genre from which their story
springs, the Turtles' relationship to females is a relatively
minor part of the mythology. The real meat lies in the relationships between males, especially between fathers and sons.
As I discussed earlier in this book, the son's quest for reconciliation with the father is a central myth of Western cultures.
Hollywood treatments of this theme usually sentimentalize
the father-son relationship and gloss over the pain it engen-
ders. Yet one of the things that is so fascinating about the
much-reviled Turtles is the extent to which the storylines
manage to tell some uncomfortable truths about fathers'
inability to connect emotionally with their sons.

The role of Splinter, the Turtles' mentor and Ninja
Master, is pivotal in this regard, and it's interesting that so
many of the Turtles' adult critics completely overlook him.
Splinter is far too old and frail to be any kind of macho role
model. His influence on the Turtles could more accurately be
characterized as a "feminizing" one. Splinter fits the model of
the nurturing mentor, the loving elder Robert Bly has called
(to considerable feminist consternation) a "male mother."
Like the idealized mothers of so many stories, he expresses a
warmth and unconditional acceptance of the Turtles, in all
their unruly goofiness. He asks only that they do their best to
live up to the ideal of self-discipline embodied in Ninja philosophy, but he never berates them when they fall short, as
they constantly do. Splinter is the father every boy secretly
longs for, but too few in our society actually have. There is an
extraordinary moment in the first *Ninja Turtles* movie when

the Turtles, thinking Splinter dead, try to conjure up his spirit. When he appears, he tells them simply and directly, "I love you all," at which point the hard-shelled heroes break down in tears. Imagine the impact of this moment on boys in our culture, so many of whom never experience this kind of honest, direct expression of feeling from their own fathers.

If Splinter embodies the loving father, the Turtles' archenemy Shredder embodies the harsh, demanding, abusive one. In the first film, Shredder exerts complete control over an underground gang of messed-up boys, contemporary descendants of *Peter Pan*'s Lost Boys, whose antisocial behaviour has made them social outcasts. They are all emotionally estranged from their families, and Shredder makes no bones about the role he plays in their lives: "This is your family," he tells them. "I am your father." But with his grinding voice, his body totally encased in armour, Shredder offers a cold, unforgiving contrast to the loving warmth of Splinter. The boys' allegiance to him is based on fear and control, not love and respect. And the Turtles' whole mission is to wrest the Lost Boys from his control, to make them see that he is a bad father because, as Splinter tells them, "Shredder cares nothing for you."

Another aspect of *Ninja Turtles* that gets short shrift is Splinter's consistenly non-violent influence. Whenever the Turtles start to run off half-cocked, unsure whether to pick a fight or gulp down a pizza, he constantly tells them things like "Fighting is the last choice of the true Ninja." In fact, self-mastery — gaining control over one's impulses — is at the heart of Splinter's teachings to his charges. Drawing on the spiritual side of the martial arts tradition, he asks them not to deny or repress their unruly, aggressive energies, but to channel them, to use them in the right way, under the proper circumstances, rather than letting themselves be ruled by them.

Developing impulse control is one of the major developmental tasks of childhood, and in our culture at least, this seems to be a more difficult task for boys. Due to a complex interplay of genetics and social conditioning, boys are more physically aggressive than girls and more likely to resolve disputes by trying to overpower an opponent. (Girls learn more readily to be good, to be "nice," qualities that may please the adults in charge but work against the girls themselves as they get older.) Helping young males develop some degree of control over these aggressive tendencies is a major preoccupation of our culture, and it is a task that largely falls to women — mothers, teachers, day-care workers. Robert Bly suggests that young males also need the loving, mentoring influence of older males in order to truly grow up. But this is a role that men in modern society have largely abdicated. In comparison to women, they play a relatively small part in raising children, and their own behaviour often provides young boys with a negative model for impulse control. What's worse, many men tend to view their own and young boys' transgressions with a boys-will-be-boys shrug. If this culture puts too much pressure on girls to be "good," to control themselves, it also gives boys too much encouragement to be "bad," to not control themselves. In the absence of truly grown-up male guidance, such as Splinter tries to provide, boys in our culture find it difficult to grow up themselves. Many never do.

Whether by intention, accident or a combination, *Ninja Turtles* mirrors some of the real dilemmas young boys must grapple with today. However, it is popular entertainment, not an instructional tool with a clear, straightforward educational message. One of adults' biggest gripes about *Ninja Turtles* and pop culture in general is that they give kids mixed messages. Whatever enlightened sentiments these shows might convey, such as Splinter's anti-violence sentiments, they seem to get cancelled out by the opposing messages. This accusation seems particularly true of *Ninja Turtles*: every movie and every TV episode end with an all-out brawl, a melee in which the Turtles get to show off their martial arts moves and overpower the enemy of the day. To most parents, this is proof that Splinter's teachings are just window dressing, that the whole show is really just an excuse for a good fight. The show's "real" message is that violence is good, fun and exciting. In a similar fashion, the first *Ninja Turtle* movie tries to have it both ways with its "father" theme. In it, Splinter tells the troubled boy Danny that "all fathers love their sons," a sentiment the film shows to be patently untrue in its exposé of the yawning gap between fathers and sons and its stinging critique of harsh, controlling fathers. The film also ends with a somewhat contrived reconciliation between Danny and his distant, work-obsessed father.

But the very term "mixed message" implies that there should be one clear message from these shows. This isn't something we demand of more sophisticated art — we don't try to reduce *Hamlet* or the novels of Dostoevsky to simple, unequivocal messages. For somewhat different reasons, I would argue that we shouldn't expect popular culture to do this either. In a sense, mixed messages are the essence of what pop culture is all about. John Fiske speaks of the fluid, contradictory character of pop culture messages, which he sees as inherent in its cut-and-run style of resistance to the existing power structures. Much of the progressive content of pop culture is not open rebellion, but "making do," creating a space for alternative images and points of view while still appearing to adhere to the established norms.

So pop culture's "mixed messages" do not so much cancel one another out as co-exist for viewers to make sense of in their own ways. This simultaneity of messages can be mightily confusing for adults, who typically misunderstand what it's all about. But it probably feels more natural to kids, since it mirrors their own more fluid mental structures. They are much less troubled by so-called contradictions than adults are. In the case of *Ninja Turtles,* they see no contradiction at all. The show appears to be having it both ways on violence partly because it mirrors exactly where the boys themselves are at. They want to fight, just as they want to give in to the urge to constantly eat pizza. But they know they shouldn't. Splinter tells them so. But since, like the Turtles themselves, they're still kids, they can't reasonably be expected to have developed a mature level of impulse control. Even Splinter doesn't expect this of them. He's tolerant and understanding of their lapses. So the "real message" of *Ninja Turtles* may be to encourage boys to keep up the struggle for self-discipline, but also to reassure them that they are still worthy of love when they fail.

Another aspect of *Ninja Turtles* that is lost on many adults is its parodic tone. The comic book started life as a send-up of superheroes like GI Joe and He-Man, and this campy sensibility still pervades it and sets it apart from those predecessors. The makers of the second *Ninja Turtles* movie responded to the criticisms of violence in the first movie with this kind of breezy parody. The film's opening brawl, for instance, is a slapstick battle in which the Turtles use every-thing from yo-yos to sandwich meats for weapons. The final blowout isn't a real fight either: the bad guys are defeated this time by rap music and breakdancing. And Shredder's ulti-mate weapons, his big scary monsters, turn out to be nothing but huge, overgrown babies who break down and bawl for their mamas.

RAINBOW RANGERS

When the Mighty Morphin Power Rangers hit the airwaves in the fall of 1993, they were immediately tagged as the heirs apparent to Turtlemania. Just as they did with the Turtles, adults denounced the Power Rangers and kids couldn't get enough of them. One New York critic pronounced it the worst series on television, but by Christmas, *Power Rangers* was the top-rated children's show. Stores' frantic efforts to keep up with the demand for Power Ranger action figures recalled the Cabbage Patch craze of the eighties. With its cheesy special effects, its resident buffoons Bulk and Skull, its bizarre father-figure Zordon (whose column-sized head is a direct steal from *The Wizard of Oz*), it's fair to say that *Mighty Morphin Power Rangers* is one of the tackier series ever to grace the public airwaves. What can you say, after all, about a show that features a gigantic helmeted pig named Porkster who threatens to devour the contents of the entire world in 48 hours? *Power Rangers* embodies nearly everything adults despise about Kid Culture. Practically every episode seems to end with a food fight or pie-throwing contest. The shows follow a formula that is so completely predictable you could set your watch by the commencement of the daily battle sequence. The Power Rangers invariably vanquish the monster of the day just shy of five minutes before each episode ends, at which point Rita, the show's main villain, gnashes her teeth and vows to defeat them next time around. *Power Rangers'* slavishness to formula may drive adults crazy, but we tend to overlook the fact that kids have a much higher tolerance, and even need, for repetition and familiarity than adults do. A large part of the show's appeal lies in its very predictability.

The big combat scenes in *Power Rangers,* which have gained it such notoriety, are more cartoon-like than most cartoons, recalling nothing so much as a grade-B fifties horror film. And, as in *Ninja Turtles,* the Power Rangers' preferred mode of fighting is martial arts. It is interesting that martial arts, with its lack of weaponry, its emphasis on inner strength, its discouragement of doing harm unnecessarily, figures so prominently in contemporary kids' entertainment, in comparison to the blowouts and shoot-'em-ups endemic in adult cop shows. And like *X-Men* and *Cadillacs and Dinosaurs,* *Power Rangers* features female characters in strong, active roles. Two of the five Rangers are girls, and the show has an even more "rainbow" cast than *X-Men,* including a black male

and an Asian female (not surprisingly, since the series is partially produced in Japan). In this sense, the *Power Rangers*
come closer than previous superheroes to reflecting the daily
reality of their young urban viewers, who come from a variety
of backgrounds and go to multi-racial schools. *Power Rangers*
also exhibits another kind of equal opportunity: like Carmen
Sandiego, "the world's greatest thief," its chief villain, Rita
Repulsa, is female. What we're seeing more and more in these
shows is greater scope for girls to break out of the confines of
the good-girl mould, to not only be active, but as bad as they
wanna be.

For all the criticism heaped on shows like *Power Rangers*
and *X-Men* by anti-violence groups, it's my contention that in
making space for female heroes and villains in previously all-
male terrain, they're helping to lead the upcoming generation
of boys and girls to a less polarized view of the sexes and their
roles. Which isn't to say there aren't limits on how far they'll
go in challenging sex roles. *Power Rangers* is actually a mass of
contradictions on this score. One episode crystallized this;
Kimberley, the pink ranger, is hoping that Tommy, the green
ranger, will ask her to the prom. While the two of them are
talking in the park, they're surprised by some of Rita's pesky
minions, the Putties, whom Kimberley proceeds to fight off
with some tough, decisive martial arts moves. But while
adults might be bothered by the juxtaposition of the "traditional" Kimberley waiting to be asked to the prom and the
strong, active Kimberley fighting off the Putties, I'm not sure
the same is true of kids. They want to have it both ways, and
pop culture is more than willing to let them have it.

BAD GIRLS / FUNNY GIRLS

Action cartoons aren't the only site of gender-role evolution
in Kid Culture. The Tiny Toons, who made their appearance
on the Fox Network in the early nineties, are pint-sized, sec-
ond-generation descendants of the original Warner Bros. car-

toon characters. The show revels in the smart-aleck humour and slam-bang anarchy we associate with the like of *Bugs Bunny* and *Daffy Duck*. But unlike the completely male-dominated Warners' universe of old, *Tiny Toons* has a female main character, Babs Bunny, who co-hosts the show with her partner Buster. Even by contemporary Saturday morning standards, *Tiny Toons* has a relative abundance of female characters — the smotheringly friendly Elmyra, the skunk Fifi and Shirley, a loon with Valley Girl inflections and a New Age belief system. In her "Saturday Morning Hell" piece, Alanna Mitchell ranked *Tiny Toons* among the "worst five" Saturday morning shows and singled it out for its "extreme sexism." Her detailed account of an episode about dating, in which Babs declares, "Never underestimate the power of Spandex," makes it abundantly clear that Mitchell finds Babs a bad role model for young girls. But being funny and being a good role model aren't always compatible objectives. For if the Ninja Turtles are, in a sense, bad boys trying to be good, Babs is a good girl who's funny because she allows herself to be bad.

Of all the popular genres, comedy has until quite recently been largely a male preserve. In comedy, women have usually been confined to the "straight man" role or have been allowed a much narrower range of comic behaviours than men. It may well be that humour will be the last barricade to fall, that the feminist revolution won't be complete until women are free to be as funny, in as great a variety of ways, as men are. As with female-centred narrative in general, part of the problem lies with women ourselves. We lack comic models to draw on and, even more fundamentally, we tend to shy away from the fairly naked use of power that comedy involves. On some level, all comic performers issue a challenge to the audience: I will make you laugh, a manipulation to which the audience willingly submits. Comedy also requires the freedom to "speak the forbidden," to violate social and ideological boundaries. Like the Trickster figure of aboriginal mythology, comedy has a quicksilver quality, refusing to be pinned down, constantly redefining itself. I think that a large part of women's difficulty in letting ourselves be funny stems from the necessity of leaving the good-girl persona behind. Funny girls are usually bad girls in one way or another. Being funny means unleashing ourselves, giving ourselves the freedom to assert power over an audience, to play with different images of ourselves, even "stereotyped" ones.

The danger in calling for the elimination of all "negative" images of women, as many feminists do, is that it often leaves us with politically correct but lifeless stories and "good" but boring heroines. More than any other form, comedy requires freedom from prescriptions and ideologies. One woman's stereotype is another woman's statement. The irony is that if we insist that all female characters be good role models, we are keeping women in the same old boxes we accuse patriarchy of doing. If women always have to be good, we can never be bad, and we probably won't end up being funny.

One of the pioneers of women's comedy in popular culture was Lucille Ball, whose entire comic persona revolved around being "bad." Virtually every episode of her enormously popular TV series of the fifties was based on the formula of Lucy trying to break the chains of female domesticity and have some fun. She does this by getting herself and her side-kick, Ethel, involved in a series of mischievous scrapes. They invariably end up getting caught, with Lucy receiving a scolding from her husband Ricky, who alternately harangues and pleads with her to "just be a wife." The running joke of the show is that Lucy is constitutionally incapable of fulfilling the role of "normal" middle-class housewife that Ricky wants her to be. I think Lucy's mischief-making can be seen as an example of the kind of everyday subversion, the "making-do," that John Fiske talks about. Her "rebellion" took the only form it could have, in the strongly conformist society of the fifties, which expected women to be the guardians of stability and morality. But not all that much has changed in this regard. In the nineties, women are still expected, by both the right and the left, to be paragons of virtue, updated versions of Goody Two-Shoes. While so-called "family values" conservatives argue that it's up to women to tame men and keep the home fires burning, leftists and environmentalists expect women to teach men to curb their violent tendencies and love the earth. But this new formula doesn't allow us any more freedom to be bad girls than the old ones did. It seems we may need Lucy every bit as much as the fifties did.

Kids today have Babs Bunny at least. Like Lucy, Babs is constantly getting into mischief, but she doesn't have to fight the same battles Lucy did with Ricky. She's not the least interested in being just a girlfriend, confined to secondary straight-man or love-interest roles. And she's Buster's wisecracking equal, his partner in mayhem. Her right to be bad, wild and funny isn't in question. One episode of the show revolves around Babs's constant tendency to get herself in trouble at home and at school. "You have no self-control!" her mother and teacher scream in exasperation — interestingly, because this is a complaint more often made about boys. *Tiny Toons* has even had its share of overtly feminist episodes, written, not surprisingly, by women. "Fields of Honey" is devoted to Babs's efforts to seek out female Toon role models. When the boys get into an argument over who is the greatest Toon character of all time, Babs realizes "I'm a girl without a guru!" and makes a time-honoured feminist complaint: "How come all the old stars were guys? Not one girl. It isn't fair! It's left me with no one to look up to." Babs sets off on a quest to find her comedy foremother, Honey, "the first female cartoon star" whom no one has seen in over 50 years. In a send-up of the movie *Field of Dreams*, a heavenly voice directs her to build her own theatre to show old Honey cartoons ("If you build it, they will watch"). Not surprisingly, Babs finds a distinct lack of interest in her quest from the male Toons; like guys everywhere, they find stories about females singularly uninteresting. But Babs's persistence and determination finally pay off when the aging Honey turns up at Babs's theatre, thrilled to discover that she's still appreciated and revered as a pioneer. In another episode, "Robin Hare," the Toons are re-enacting the Robin Hood story. Babs starts out as Maid Marian, then gets fed up, exclaiming, "A girl can't be a helpless damsel all the time!" She decides to take on more active roles and winds up dueling with the Sheriff of Nottingham and even auditioning for the role of Hamlet ("to Babs or not to Babs").

Babs is not the only one of the Tiny Toons to thumb her nose at convention. Rebellion and anti-authoritarian attitudes — values that since the fifties have been associated with adolescence — have been gradually filtering down to the preadolescent years, much to many adults' dismay. *Tiny Toons* has run its share of the "message" themes *de rigueur* in children's entertainment — episodes about saving the environment and the dangers of smoking have appeared in the series, for instance. But much more of the humour is of the subversive, irreverent type I talked about in chapter two. In one episode, which plays out almost like a Beleaguered Animators' Manifesto, the Tiny Toons are confronted by a fusty crusader representing the Adult Coalition Against Cartoon Silliness. Vowing "Reality shall rule!" she threatens to clean up all the show's loony antics with a gigantic vacuum cleaner. The Toons argue against censorship and plead for the freedom they feel is essential to true comedy. By a variety of stratagems — including pummeling the Ms. Do-Gooder with an avalanche of cartoon anvils — they emerge victorious and reclaim their subversive souls. Like any self-respecting Toon, the censor lady is unharmed by her brush with the anvils, and the episode ends happily as she discovers her own "tooniness" and goes bouncing off into Wackyland, the *Tiny Toons'* version of utopia. This anti-authoritarianism is even more explicit in the *Tiny Toons'* spinoff *Animaniacs,* which premiered in the fall of 1993. Episodes of *Animaniacs* typically end with a "Wheel of Morality" segment, which openly mocks the moral lessons children's programs are expected to deliver. Typical "morals for today": "If at first you don't succeed, blame it on your parents" and "Vote early, vote often." Where *Mad* magazine was considered subversive for introducing nine- and ten-year-olds to satire, the new generation of cartoons is doing the same for viewers as young as three and four. As in *Mad,* pop culture and consumerism are frequent targets of *Tiny Toon* parodies. And like everyone else, they took their own jabs at the Teenage Mutant Ninja Turtles — "Immature Radioactive Samurai Slugs." Like *Sesame Street* and so many other contemporary kids' shows, the humour in *Tiny Toons* is designed to work on two levels: adults and older kids get the satirical points, the in-jokes and pop culture references, which go right over the heads of younger children. When I watched the Samurai Slugs episodes with a five-year-old friend of my daughter's, it was clear he had no clue that the show was making fun of his beloved Ninja Turtles. But he enjoyed the whole episode as a good story nonetheless.

POSTMODERN TOONS

Another thing adults get from checking out a few episodes of *Tiny Toons* — whether they're aware of it or not — is a quick course in postmodern concepts like intertextuality. This term has been coined by contemporary deconstruction theorists to describe the ways in which literary and pop culture "texts" constantly draw on one another. *Tiny Toons* is a veritable textbook (no pun intended) of intertextuality, with its parodies of advertising and other TV shows, caricatures of well-known Hollywood figures (including its own executive producer, Steven Spielberg, who turns up from time to time as a character), and frequent references to its own Warner Bros. cartoon antecedents. In one episode I counted in the space of five minutes references to two movies (*Wizard of Oz* and *A*

Streetcar Named Desire), caricatures of John Wayne and Katharine Hepburn and appearances by old Warner Bros. character Elmer Fudd, as well as the Warners' corporate logo itself. Another episode managed to combine in rapid succession parodies of *The Simpsons* (Babs as Marge baking cupcakes), PBS icon Fred Rogers ("Yeah, yeah, it's a beautiful day in my neighbourhood. So what?") and Arnold Schwarzenegger as a muscle-bound, not-too-bright Teutonic lifeguard.

This stance of irony and self-awareness echoes a related theme found in many contemporary cartoons and other children's entertainments: the idea of alternative realms and states of reality. With the rise of computers, video games and virtual reality, the upcoming generation is already far more familiar with the notion of alternative realities than their print-based, linear-thinking parents. Those of us who grew up prior to the sixties had the idea of conformity to a single, narrowly defined reality branded on our brains. The political movements and the drug culture of the sixties may have begun to dismantle this mind-set. But kids today already know that you don't need chemical substances to experience altered states of reality. Computers, cartoons and multimedia entertainments are helping them find new ways of opening Aldous Huxley's "doors of perception." In the case of *Tiny Toons*, this is literally true: One of the Toons' favourite stratagems, when they're in a jam or want a change of scene, is to paint a door and walk right through it. Their home base of Acme Acres has its own parallel universe, Wackyland ("Home Surreal Home"), where the Toons experience bizarre alterations of reality, often initiated by GoGo, a character of indeterminate sex and species who can replicate and change shape at will. Another popular kids' show, *Where in the World Is Carmen Sandiego?*, takes this idea even further. The storylines of this show make no pretense of taking place in a "real" or even "imaginary" reality, but in virtual reality — what computer aficionados call "cyberspace." In each episode, the adolescent detective characters are catapulted instantaneously via computer to far-flung spots on the globe, where they try to track down the notorious thief and world-class escape artist Carmen Sandiego. This computer bent of the show isn't surprising, considering that the concept was derived from popular educational software of the same name. In their different ways, shows like *Tiny Toons* and *Carmen Sandiego* bolster Marsha Kinder's thesis that popular culture is preparing the next generation to function comfortably in a fragmented but computer-literate postmodern world.

The marvel of animation has always been its freedom to play with reality this way. But the new crop of cartoons goes further in the way they constantly comment on and draw attention to the "Toon illusion," the animation process itself. Earlier generations of kids were encouraged to suspend disbelief and watch cartoons as if they were "really happening." In my years as a playwright, I've heard endless discussions among theatre artists about how to break down the "fourth wall," the invisible barrier between the stage and the audience. But the fourth wall actually crumbled long ago in many areas of Kid Culture. *Tiny Toons* devoted an entire episode to its own (supposed) genesis, showing the "birth" of Babs and Buster as the animator (himself an animated character) sketches them on a sheet. The show also gets considerable comic mileage out of simultaneously using and sending up hoary old cartoon conventions like exploding cakes and falling anvils. One episode has Elmer Fudd delivering a lecture on "cartoon logic," which includes demonstrations of walking on thin air. On another occasion, Plucky Duck gets trapped in a "wild take." While he's having a standard-issue cartoon fit, one of his eyeballs bulges out so far its sucks in the rest of his body. He spends the rest of the episode bouncing around as a giant eyeball while Buster and Babs search frantically for a cure in a medical textbook entitled *Toon Trauma*.

But I wonder if it's possible that we're reaching the limits of all this hip irony in children's culture. I argued earlier in this book that kids' humour, like Kid Culture in general, is becoming less innocent, more adult, and that the line between children's and adults' entertainment is becoming less distinct. No matter how much it may dismay adults, kids nowadays are more knowing about the world and sexuality, less sheltered from the harsher realities of modern life. But they are still kids. I don't believe that kids are natural cynics. There is still a fragility and openness that sets children apart from adults. And because their identities are still evolving and they have so little control over their own lives, children do need points of reference. They need to believe in something. The problem with so much self-referential postmodernism is that it can lead to a dead end where nothing is taken seriously, nothing is allowed to matter. For all its edge, its hip humour and pop culture references, *Tiny Toons* still follows a fairly classic formula of traditional narrative structures and pie-in-the-face comedy. The friendships between the continuing characters are all-important and form the basis for most of the storylines. In this light, it's interesting to compare *Tiny Toons* with its spinoff series *Animaniacs*. Both shows are produced by Steven Spielberg's Amblin Entertainment and have essentially the same creative team. But a decision was clearly made to go for a higher irony quotient with *Animaniacs*, and the result is, to my mind at least, a children's show almost completely skewed to adult tastes. Episodes of *Animaniacs* are often little more than an empty bag of postmodern tricks, with little in the way of storyline and a nonstop parade of caricatures of adult celebrities like talk-show hosts and movie reviewers. The show is fronted by a trio of characters with identical, vacuous expressions — the "Warner Brothers and their sister Dot" — whose name carries self-referentiality (not to mention self-promotion) to new extremes. Like the Tiny Toons, the Warner Brothers and their pals are irreverent and mischievous, but there's a mean-spiritedness, a lack of warmth about the Animaniacs that wasn't there in their predecessors.

One episode in the series, "Bumbi," is a takeoff on Walt Disney's *Bambi*. In it, one of the continuing characters, Slappy Squirrel, takes her nephew Skippy to see the movie and, like children everywhere, he breaks down and cries at the point where Bambi's mother is killed by the hunters. But instead of comforting Skippy, Slappy upbraids him for being silly: "It's only a movie ... . No one ever really gets hurt in cartoons." But her nephew is unconsolable, and Slappy finally takes him to meet the "actress" who played Bambi's mother (an old pal of hers) to prove that that the "death" was just pretend. While this cartoon-within-a-cartoon format, calling attention to the "Toon illusion," is standard fare in current animated series, what bothered me about the episode was the belittling of Skippy's feelings, which were "real" to him even though he knew full well the story was not. The story of Bambi, of course, has always elicited powerful responses in children, particularly the fear of being abandoned, of losing the beloved parent. But children watching the Bumbi episode get the same, quite un-funny message Slappy gives Skippy: It's "silly" to cry over a story, to take it seriously, to let anything matter that much.

Meanwhile, in the middle of this sea of hip knowingness in children's entertainment sits Barney, like an island of gooey, earnest sincerity. The quality Barney most singularly lacks is irony. There is no doubt in his beloved fans' minds that he means absolutely everything he says, that his constant expressions of love and caring are completely genuine. In the more cynical adult world, of course, Barney has become an icon of a decidedly different sort. The I Hate Barney movement may have reached its nadir of utterly tasteless hilarity with the publication of *Final Exit for Barney*, a takeoff on the notorious how-to manual of assisted suicide. But as much as *Barney and*

Friends might look to adults like the kids' show from hell, or a satirical skit that the old SCTV series might have cooked up, small children embrace it wholeheartedly and see in Barney's openness and innocence a mirror of their own. And the show's phenomenal popularity may well be a kind of cultural signal that the pendulum has swung far enough, that kids still need to believe in something unreservedly.

Jerome and Dorothy Singer have come to Barney's defence, calling the show "nearly a model of what a pre-school show should be." But the frustrating thing about Barney's success is that its themes of fostering imagination and building self-esteem have been done and are being done much better elsewhere. *Fred Penner's Place,* for example, a gentle-toned Canadian pre-school show that also runs on the U.S. Nickelodeon channel, covers a lot of the same territory with fresher storylines and more varied musical offerings than the hackneyed fare of a typical Barney episode. And despite the fact that it runs on educational TV , there's little to separate Barney from his counterparts on commercial TV in terms of marketing spinoffs. I think that in some ways Barney represents the worst of both worlds: commercialized, formula entertainment without the sass and verve of a *Tiny Toons,* "educational" content minus the imaginative spark of *Sesame Street.* Then again, I'm an adult. What do I know? In Kid Culture, kids' tastes rule, and Barney is incontrovertible evidence of that fact.

CHAPTER EIGHT

Beyond Fear and Loathing: Learning to Live with Kid Culture

AS WE MOVE THROUGH the final decade of the 20th century, many adults seem locked into a fear-and-loathing response to KidCulture. Throughout this book I've argued against this response and tried to show how much of it is based on a misunderstanding of pop culture and how it works. But the main problem I see with this attitude toward Kid Culture is that it's a dead end. It takes us nowhere except to become one more in a long line of missed opportunities for dialogue between the generations.

The sad thing is that pop culture, which seems to have driven such a wedge between adults and children, also presents such a fruitful opportunity for connection between them. To a certain extent, the war between the generations is inevitable, normal and necessary. But some of the roots of the deep generational estrangement we see in our society, the barrier which becomes a brick wall in adolescence, may well lie in the wholesale disdain adults exhibit toward children's culture. It's possible that if we work a little harder at building bridges of understanding with our kids right from their earliest years, this generational chasm can at least be made narrower.

But just how do we learn to live with Kid Culture? I think a large part of the battle for adults lies in becoming more aware of our own preconceived notions and how they shape our responses to children. For instance, in an earlier chapter I discussed the all-too-common adult tendency to dismiss children's world and concerns out of hand, and compared it to the "developmental disdain" older children feel for younger ones. This adult version of developmental disdain has its roots in our reluctance to identify ourselves with childish needs and tastes, our need to believe that we have outgrown such things. But on a deeper level, it's a subtle form of child-hating, a disowning of the children we ourselves once were. These prejudices shape adults' whole approach to children's culture. For many of us, the view that if kids like something it must be of low quality has become almost axiomatic. We expect to find junk, and so it's not surprising when we do.

The widespread sentiment that childhood "ain't what it used to be" also frames our response to Kid Culture. While there's undeniable truth to the idea that modern children are being robbed of a real childhood, it's also true that our children are not growing up in the same world we did, that society has changed and is changing. Modern childhood no longer looks so carefree and innocent to us, but that is largely a nostalgia-tinged myth. There has always been an underside to childhood, a darker country of pain, powerlessness and humiliation that few adults would choose to voluntarily revisit, or to even acknowledge its existence. This, what Alice Miller calls "banished knowledge," is what makes so many adults turn away from the real world children face, and seek solace in an idealized of childhood of yesteryear, or at least the belief that our own childhood "wasn't that bad."

Nostalgia for the past, for the childhood that probably never was, has a powerful grip on the collective psyche. One pervasive, current version of it is the widespread belief that we live in a time of unprecedented violence, and that the popular media — naturally — are to blame. Yet outside of wartime situations, the violence of past times was largely hidden in the home. Much of what we have now come to call "domestic violence" was directed against children themselves, in the form of physical, sexual and emotional abuse. The great irony is that, for all that adults persist in believing that children's entertainment should be innocent and squeaky-clean, large numbers of children, past and present, have had an intimate acquaintance with violence and other forms of cruelty. Personally, I find it remarkable that we can spend so much time and energy talking about violence on TV, and comparatively little time talking about the fact that striking children for disciplinary purposes is still legal in most of the world, and that the majority of adults still believe the use of of physical punishment is appropriate and necessary. In the end, it's impossible to say with certainty whether the present is more violent than past times. What is certain is that much of the hidden violence of the past has come out of the woodwork and spilled into the open, where it can finally be seen and named. Private violence has become public violence, and my personal view is that the violent imagery that pervades popular culture nowadays is as much a reflection of this reality as it is a cause.

Coming to terms with Kid Culture also means choosing our battles more wisely. Despite all the focus the anti-violence movement has brought to the content of children's programming, my own reading of the evidence convinces me that the real problem is the amount of TV kids watch, regardless of content. The mesmerizing, sedating effects of TV are undeniable. Studies which suggest that kids who are heavy TV viewers have less developed imaginations and play skills are cause for real concern. Though I may have a more sanguine view of pop culture than many adults, I don't advocate an unlimited diet of it. Television can stimulate kids' imaginations and expand their horizons, but it's not a substitute for life experience, and, in the absence of other kinds of stimulation, it can shrink their universe as well. I argued earlier that that kids need a substantial amount of TV-free time to process the stories and images they are exposed to. They need time to play, time to use their bodies, time to relate to other people — time, quite simply, to live life. Much of the debate about television assumes that it asserts an almost irresistable control over the household. But I'm convinced that it's both possible and necessary to create a different climate, to treat TV as a useful tool, a source of entertainment that we can control.

Limiting the amount of TV kids can watch also means they have to make choices, to decide what they like, to discriminate rather than just watching whatever happens to be on. But I think we should strive to leave the choice of what to watch largely up to kids themselves. One practical reason for this is that the shows they aren't allowed to watch invariably turn out to be the ones they want to watch the most. This sets up the familiar forbidden-fruit situation, in which the denied object assumes a greater allure, a kind of charge that's directly proportional to the negativity the parent invests it with. Of course, the question of what kind of programs are appropriate for children of different ages has to be taken into account. One of our jobs as parents is to protect our kids from experiences that may be too frightening or overwhelming for them to cope with. Yet one Toronto survey found that children as young as five or six were watching dark, disturbing films like *Silence of the Lambs* on video. It has become commonplace in the current debate to call for government-imposed controls in order to protect children from the evils of TV violence. In his defense of Canada's new anti-violence code, for instance, CRTC Chairman Keith Spicer has frequently described TV violence as a "medical problem" that harms children and which justifies such a censorship-oriented approach. But given that a major target of the code is cartoons and other programs aimed specifically at kids, it's worth asking just who is it we're trying to protect here? Children, or ourselves from the bullies and murderers we're so convinced pop culture is turning them into? If protection of children themselves is our aim, maybe we should be more concerned about the frightening acts of violence and scenes of war kids routinely witness on the news, for example. These images clearly cause them more anxiety than the slapstick violence of the average cartoon show.

Giving kids an age-appropriate degree of control over their choices from the Kid Culture menu is only part of the story. An indispensable corollary is to engage with them about their choices. One of the most respected critics of children's television, Action for Children's Television founder Peggy Charren, favours this approach over content controls because, as she told one interviewer, "The possibility of censorship bothers me at least as much as what children are watching." Charren recommends that parents view TV with what she calls "TLC": Talk, Look and Choose. Talk with children about TV, look at it with them when possible, choose for them when they're little and with them as they get older. Charren's snappy acronym seems to me as good a guideline as any for fostering the kind of media literacy so much in vogue these days. Helping our kids develop a critical perspective is one of the best gifts we can give them, and irreverence is, in the end, a far better teacher than censorship.

The preschool years aren't too early to begin engaging in dialogue with kids about pop culture. Of course, very young children are more likely to simply recount the story or list their favourite elements, rather than give anything resembling an adult's idea of an opinion. But the exercise itself is what's important. The earlier kids are treated as though their ideas matters, the more critical and independent-minded they will be. Talking with children doesn't, however, include what I referred to as the "sneer tactic" in the opening chapter of this book: sitting back in smug judgement, being blindly critical of everything they like. We also have to keep in mind that the younger children are, the more their thought processes differ from adults'. Even if they arrive at what we consider the "right" answer or opinion, they may get there by an unexpected or circuitous route, and that's a journey we have to allow them to take. Also, carrying out this dialogue can be a trickly business for modern parents, many of whom tend to err on the side of over-involvement with our children. A buttinsky parent who wants to "share" everything can be every bit as oppressive as the authoritarian one who tries to forbid everything. The true dance of parenthood probably resides in a savvy response to the contradictory message our kids throw at us as a matter of course: "I need you — Go away."

Admittedly, Charren's approach assumes that parents are actually on the scene often enough to "talk, look and choose" with their kids. Some media critics routinely dismiss this kind of approach because "parents today have no time" to monitor what their kids are watching. There is growing interest in various kinds of absentee monitoring systems, most notably the V-chip, a device which would allow parents to block out incoming programs with a high "V" for violence rating. With devices like the V-chip, as Keith Spicer rather blithely put it, "the parents become the censors." What I find dismaying about all this is the unspoken acceptance of the fact that, for all our talk of family and "quality time," many adults don't really have much meaningful contact with their children. We have to regulate our children's viewing by remote control because, in so many cases, we're simply not there. It's as if on a wholesale societal level we've given up on our adult roles, given up on the family as a site of meaningful human interaction. The reasons for this flight from adult responsibilty are manifold: economic pressures, especially in single-parent families, are stretching some parents' coping abilities to the limit. Large numbers of adults in our society simply carry too much emotional damage from their own upbringing to be much help to their children. Other preoccupations, such as building a career, can divert parents' time and energy away from their children's lives. But whatever the cause, the consequences are the same: large numbers of kids are adrift, without much in the way of loving attention and guidance from adults.

This wholesale parental abdication is itself turning up more and more as a subject in movies and TV. I've already discussed the scathing critique of the adult world in the dark teen comedy *Heathers.* Some of the most popular family films of recent years also explore versions of this theme, albeit with considerably less satirical awareness. Movies like *Home Alone* and *Curly Sue* are populated with kids who take on adult responsibilities, who don't really seem to need adults at all because, like children depicted in medieval paintings, they're actually pint-sized adults themselves. In one sense, of course, these films are so popular because they reflect a typical child's power fantasy: "I can make it on my own — I don't need you." But they may also be reflecting a much more ominous adult fantasy: "The kids are all right — they don't need us." Which is one way of justifying our own failure to offer support and guidance, to be there for them. Canadian children's author and playwright Dennis Foon points out that TV itself is taking on more and more of the parent's role in society, instilling values and providing children — however inadequately — with a sense of family and community. The irony of this is that in railing against the evils of TV, adults seek to deny kids the very thing they turn to in an attempt to fill the vacuum created by absentee adults.

There seems to be another, even more pessimistic assumption underlying adult hostility to Kid Culture, a sense that we have already washed our hands of this generation, written them off as a bunch of hopeless couch potatoes and illiterate video heads. This is nothing new, of course. Each new generation is held up as a symbol of the wholesale decline of civilization. My own contemporaries, the radicals and counterculture types who came of age in the sixties and early seventies, were certainly seen in this light. But the current despair seems more profound, and more ominous. As Benjamin Barber says in a *Harper's* magazine article on the education system, "We have given up on the kids because we have given up on the future, perhaps because it looks too multicolored or too dim or too hard." Yet as much as it may be a cliche to say it, youth is the future, and no society which hopes to survive can afford to give up on own young.

MEETING THE MILLENIUM

Though the vast bulk of what's produced in TV, film and pop music appears to simply reinforce the social and political status quo, there is in every medium an edge, a place where new values and images are continually bubbling up from the collective psyche and being transmitted to wider audiences. Throughout this book I've tried to show this process at work, particularly with regard to female-centred stories. But there are numerous other examples to point to. Openly gay superheroes like *Alpha Flight's* Northstar and *Flash's* Pied Piper have been steadily infiltrating the world of action comics for well over a decade. Super Shamou, a popular superhero created by Inuit broadcaster Peter Tapatai, inspires northern children with his message of native self-respect and the dangers of solvent sniffing. And one of the most striking examples of pop culture's progressive potential is the ever-expanding *Star Trek* universe. Right from the original sixties TV show down through its most recent incarnations, *Star Trek* has been a pop culture trailblazer, celebrating diversity, upholding the importance of community and spreading the idea that human relationships, not technology, will be paramount in the world of the future.

I think there's an argument to be made that far more than political movements, it's pop culture that does the real work of spreading the message of social change. But we should be wary of efforts to tame its vitality and make it subservient to didactic ends. However lofty its moral purpose, the best art, popular or otherwise, allows the audience to discover the message for themselves. And I agree with John Fiske that there needs to be a fairly realistic correlation between the world as it is and the world depicted in pop culture texts:

> However we might wish to change the social meanings and textual representation of, say, women or non-white races, such changes can only be slow and evolutionary, not radical and revolutionary, *if the texts are to remain popular.*" (My emphasis)

By the same token, a violence- and stereotype-free popular culture is probably not possible or even desirable. With popular art we are often in the realm of myth, of larger-than-life rather than "real" life, which explains much of its powerful appeal for children. Few of the educators and child-development professionals who are so critical of Kid Culture have much of an understanding or appreciation of this myth-giving function. The "positive role models" these experts are so fond of calling for need to have this mythic, larger-than-life dimension if they're to work in a pop culture context.

One of the most serious criticisms levelled at pop culture is that it homogenizes and ultimately destroys the local cultures with which it comes in contact. This is a longstanding issue in a country like Canada, sitting right next door to the U.S. and its huge entertainment industry, fighting a constant battle to maintain its own distinctive cultural identity. Since the advent of television, cultural survival has become a complex and pressing concern worldwide. But the flip side of this coin is that pop culture may also be helping to foster a truly global sense of community. Anita Sheth, a Toronto sociologist and media analyst, argues that "the culture of the Word isolates us" whereas "the culture of the Image binds us." Sheth's views are rooted in the fact that she grew up in India, a culture which honours the image. In her view, TV and other image-based media actually help to build a sense of community by exposing us to a panoply of experience beyond our everyday lives, which fosters an appreciation of differences, of alternate views of reality. She points to ads featuring starving children in the Third World as an example. These ads make a deep impression on Western children, whose immediate impulse is often to race to the phone and pledge a donation. They respond with an instinctive, boundless compassion that contrasts sharply with adults, who cynically dismiss the ads' blatant manipulativeness. I've seen a similar dynamic at work with kids, who in their pre-teen years often start to develop an appetite for tabloid-style talk shows like *Geraldo* and *Oprah*. These shows exert a powerful attraction because they serve as part of kids' introduction to the larger world beyond home and school. The adults in their lives are often contemptuous of the *True Confession* antics and the freak-show atmosphere of these shows. But time and again I've seen kids come away from watching them with genuine concern and compassion for the guests, no matter how bizarre their confessions or aberrant their behaviour.

To many adults, of course, it's nothing short of appalling that so much of kids' information about the world is filtered through this multi-track pop culture panorama. It certainly lends some credence to Camille Paglia's theory, which I cited earlier, that we are in the midst of a "repaganization" process — a historic swing of the pendulum away from the primacy of the written word toward the image and the spoken word. Many see this shift in near-apocalyptic terms. But civilization did not begin with the printing press, and I don't think it's true that the resurgence of oral and image-based culture means an inevitable, wholesale abandonment of literacy. But it probably is accurate to say that literacy and the written word are assuming a new position on the cultural spectrum, and will play a different — still evolving— role for upcoming generations. We should keep in mind that for the young, this shift that we elders find so threatening is simply the normal course of events. They will be shaped, like we were, by the culture they grow up in. And popular culture is arguably doing a better job of preparing them to meet the millenium than we can hope to do.

It may be that the thing that most disturbs adults about Kid Culture is something that most are only dimly conscious of — namely, the fact that it is part of an historic shift in the power balance between adults and children. I've already explored the anti-authoritarian current that runs right through modern-day pop culture from *Mad* to *The Simpsons*, and some of its roots in even older forms of childhood culture like schoolyard rhymes. These challenges to adult authority may be effective, or they may be just so much blowing off steam. But there are many ways in which modern pop culture is actively helping to undermine adult authority. For example, as John Fiske points out, television often shows adults in their "backstage" or private mode of behavior, and thus exposes their fallibility to children.

> The mystique of adulthood, by which adults maintain their discipline over children, is exposed ... and thus the naturalness of their power is called into question. Children may be less amenable to social discipline in the television age simply because television exposes the imperfections of adulthood to them.

So while many adults continue to insist that pop culture rots children's minds and enslaves them to consumerism, I believe it's also helping to create the conditions, on a global scale, for the last great liberation movement of this century — that of children.

No term quite fits the bill for this movement, however. "Kids' liberation" smacks of the unrestrained freedom of the sixties, a lifestyle which many radicals of the period tried to live out in the way they raised their children. But this "liberation" didn't much take into account the particular nature or needs of childhood, and often ended up being more liberating for the adults than for the kids themselves. The more legalistic "Children's Rights" model of the seventies and eighties is a more useful but still not quite adequate attempt to graft an adult-oriented model on the complex reality of childhood. What I think is beginning to emerge now is a deeper understanding of that reality — how different it is from adults', but how equally valid and worthy of respect. With this understanding comes a historic redefinition of children as persons in their own right: people who are different from adults, who need the protection of adults and cannot act with the same degree of autonomy as they do, but who have innate dignity and rights as human beings. It's a great irony that we live in a culture that so idealizes "youth," but that shows so little interest in and respect for the real lives of children. If Kid Culture is helping to bring about a world in which children are truly valued, where their needs are at the centre of the culture where they belong, then more power to it.

NOTES

p. 9, "a modern-day Virgin Mary ...": Isabel Vincent. "Queen of the Shorties," *Globe and Mail,* December 17, 1992, p. C2.

p. 21, "the autonomy they will exercise ...": Thomas Hurka. "Fifth Column: Thomas Hurka Examines the Limitations on the Rights of Children," *Globe and Mail,* October 23, 1990, p. A20.

p. 26, "the folk poetry ...": Edith Fowke. *Sally Go Round the Sun.* Toronto: McClelland & Stewart, 1969, p. 6.

p. 30, "In one study ...": "Abused Children Have Lower IQs, U.S. Study Finds," *Toronto Star,* February 18, 1991, p. A5.

p. 31, "create a miniature ...": Dorothy G. Singer and Jerome L. Singer. *The House of Make-Believe: Play and the Developing Imagination.* Cambridge, Mass.: Harvard University Press, 1990, p. 42.

p. 32, "serves an important ...": Ibid., p. 44.

p. 32, "Most of the great ...": Alison Lurie. *Don't Tell the Grown-ups: Subversive Children's Literature.* Boston: Little, Brown, 1990, p. xi.

p. 33, "to transform painful ...": Martha Wolfenstein. *Children's Humor.* Glencoe, Ill.: The Free Press, 1954, p. 18.

p. 36, "Miracle Whip": Elizabeth MacCallum. "Munsch's Formula Is Less Successful on Other Levels," *Globe and Mail,* May 16, 1992, p. C1.

p. 37, "in a realm ...": Camille Paglia and Neil Postman. "She Wants Her TV! He Wants His Book!" *Harper's,* March, 1991, p. 47.

p. 37, "multilayered, multitrack ...": Ibid., p. 47.

p. 38, "The only defence ...": Ibid., p. 54.

p. 39, "They're heavily influenced ...": Patricia Lush. "Parents Passing on Playful Memories," *Globe and Mail,* April 7, 1992, p. A6.

p. 40, "Moralists, by nature ...": Bruno Bettelheim. "Suffer Little Children to Watch TV," *Guardian Weekly,* March 25, 1990, p. 21.

p. 41, "the supreme triumph ...": Howard Zinn. *A People's History of the United States.* New York: Harper and Row, 1980, p. 293.

p. 49, "I have crossed ...": Vivian Gussin Paley. *Boys and Girls: Superheroes in the Doll Corner.* Chicago: University of Chicago Press, 1984, p. 104.

p. 49, "the five-year-old's passion ...": Ibid., p. ix.

p. 49, "boys like ..." Ibid., p. 109.

p. 50, "When the children ...": Ibid.., p. ix.

p. 50, "an unavoidable conclusion ...": Ibid, p. 105.

p. 54, "A surprising number ...": Michael Smith. "Dissecting Deters Female Scientists, Conference Is Told," *Toronto Star,* August 6, 1993, p. A8.

p. 59, "rented gigolo ...": Marnie Jackson. "Gals and Dolls: The Moral Value of 'Bad' Toys," *This Magazine,* December/January, 1991, p. 35

p. 64, "The boys never ...": Paley, op. cit., p. 113.

p. 66, "Woman: symbolism ...": Joseph Campbell. *The Hero with a Thousand Faces.* Princeton, N.J.: Princeton University Press, 1949, p. 416.

p. 67, "marked": Deborah Tannen. "Marked Women," *Globe and Mail,* July 17, 1993, p. D5.

p. 69, "I'm very aware ...": "A League of Their Own," *Maclean's,* March 29, 1993, p. 39.

p. 69, "Everyone talks about ...": Bruce Westbrook. "Hollywood Is

Where the Girls Aren't," *Globe and Mail*, December 17, 1993, p. B3.

p. 70, "You have to have boys ...": Bill Carter. "Saturday Morning TV Is a Boy's World," *Globe and Mail*, April 16, 1991, p. C3.

p. 70, "When there are a boy and ...": Salem Alaton. "That's not all, Folks!", *Globe and Mail*, July 4, 1992, p. C11.

p. 79, "... where it is *de rigueur* ...": Paulette Jiles. "In Search of the Picara," *This Magazine*, December, 1985, p. 31.

p. 80-81, "One cannot make up ...", "as-yet-unwritten ...", "Within the quest plot ...": Carolyn Heilbrun. "What Was Penelope Unweaving?", *Hamlet's Mother and Other Women*. New York: Columbia University Press, 1990, p. 108.

p. 87, "father who wants ...": Bruno Bettelheim. *The Uses of Enchantment*. New York: Vintage Books, 1975, p. 245.

p. 97, "fractured, in some state ...": Aljean Harmetz. *The Making of the Wizard of Oz*. New York: Delta Books, 1977, p. 312.

p. 103, "That broke the rule ...": *Maclean's*, op. cit., p. 38.

p. 108, "Marc Lépine ...", "play war ...": André Picard. "Plastic Guns, GI Joe Gone to Graveyard," *Globe and Mail*, December 6, 1991, p. A 7.

p. 109, "teach her kids ...": "Thea-Retically," *Entertainment Weekly*, February 4, 1994, p. 13.

p. 109, "Is the current ...": Liam Lacey. "Bodies of Evidence," *Globe and Mail*, August 7, 1993, p. C1.

p. 109, "distracts attention ...": Todd Gitlin. "Imagebusters: The Hollow Crusade against TV Violence," *Utne Reader*, May/June, 1994, p. 92.

p. 109, "We can't seem ...": Terry Rakolta on *Between the Lines*, TVOntario, broadcast November 10, 1993.

p. 110, "We're all a bit hypocritical ...": Bronwyn Drainie. "Biff! Bam! Pow! Click. The Push to Turn off TV Violence," *Globe and Mail*, June 23, 1990, p. C1.

p. 111, "trash": Peter A. Soderbergh "The Stratemeyer Strain: Educators and the Juvenile Series Book, 1900-1980," *Only Connect: Readings on Children's Literature*, Sheila Egoff et al. (eds.) Toronto: Oxford University Press, 1980, pp. 63-73.

p. 114, "extraordinarily inappropriate ...": "Parents Riled by PBS Fund Raising," *Globe and Mail*, March 20, 1993, p. C6.

p. 115, "Children believe ...": Alaton. op. cit., p. C1.

p. 115, "If all the violence ...": "Million Sign Teen's Petition against TV Violence," *Globe and Mail*, December 5, 1992, p. A8.

p.117, "beating up on ...": Isabel Vincent. "Censors Defy Tradition to Box in TV Crime," *Globe and Mail*, August 13, 1993, p. C2.

p. 118, "Freedman claims ...": Henry Mietkiewicz. "Studies link TV Violence and Viewer Aggression," *Toronto Star*, January 16, 1993, p. G8.

p. 118, "We never counted ...": Kevin Marron. "Net of Specialists Unable to Snare Two Young Killers," *Globe and Mail*, December 27, 1991, p. A6.

p. 118, "The difference between ...": Mira Friedlander. "Challenging the Root Causes of Violent Behaviour," *Toronto Star*, May 6, 1993, p. C6.

p. 119, "watching life ...": Ashley Montagu. *Growing Young*. New York: McGraw-Hill, 1981, p. 142.

p. 121, "the highest level ...": Rhéal Séguin. "TV Rates High on Violence Scale," *Globe and Mail*, June 4, 1994, p. A1.

p. 122, "happy violence ...": Alaton. op. cit., p. C11.

p. 123, "CRTC Chairman Keith Spicer ...": Greg Quill. "GI Joe's a Goner under New TV Rules," *Toronto Star*, October 31, 1993, p. A4.

p. 125, "to facilitate ...": Marsha Kinder. *Playing with Power in Movies, Television and Video Games*. Berkeley, Calif.: University of California Press, 1991, p. 61.

p. 127, "failed to produce ...": John Fiske. *Understanding Popular Culture*. London, Routledge, 1989, p. 162.

p. 128, "turn cultural commodities ...": Ibid., p. 66.

p. 130, "extreme sexism ..." Alanna Mitchell. "Saturday Morning Hell," *Globe and Mail*, April 3, 1993, p. C1.

p. 131, "one long toy commercial": David Bianculli. "TV's Worst Series One Long Toy Commercial," *Toronto Star*, December 21, 1993, p. B5.

p. 131, "There's been a complete ...": Mitchell, op. cit., p. C1.

p. 155, "nearly a model ...": Jon Lender. "Researchers Bash the Barney-bashers,": *Toronto Star*, October 26, 1993, p. E8.

p. 159, "one Toronto survey ...": Barbara Aarsteinsen. "Brutal Images Bombard Kids," *Toronto Star*, December 5, 1992, p. A2.

p. 160, "The possibility of censorship ...": Peggy Charren on "Prime Time Violence," *Investigative Reports*, Arts and Entertainment Network, March 17, 1994.

p. 161, "the parents become ...": Keith Spicer on *Between the Lines*, op. cit.

p. 162, "Canadian children's author ...": Sid Adilman. "Playwright's World Is Millions of Kids," *Toronto Star*, May 2, 1994, p. B4.

p. 163, "We have given up ...": Benjamin Barber. "America Skips School: Why We Talk So Much about Education and Do So Little," *Harper's*, November, 1993, p. 46.

p. 164, "However we might wish ...": Fiske, op. cit., p. 133.

p. 164, "the culture of the Word ...": Anita Sheth, personal communication.

p. 166, "The mystique of adulthood ...": Fiske, op. cit., p. 157.

BIBLIOGRAPHY

Ariès, Philippe. *Centuries of Childhood: A Social History of Family Life.* Translated from the French by Robert Baldick. New York: Vintage Books, 1962.

Bassoff, Evelyn S. *Mothering Ourselves: Help and Healing for Adult Daughters.* New York: Penguin Books, 1991.

Bettelheim, Bruno. *The Uses of Enchantment: The Meaning and Importance of Fairy Tales.* New York: Vintage Books, 1975.

Bly, Robert. *Iron John: A Book about Men.* New York: Vintage Books, 1990.

Campbell, Joseph. *The Hero with a Thousand Faces.* Princeton, N.J.: Princeton University Press, 1949.

Carlsson-Paige, Nancy, and Levin, Diane E. *Who's Calling the Shots? How to Respond Effectively to Children's Fascination with War Play and War Toys.* Philadelphia, Pa.: New Society Publishers, 1990.

Egoff, Sheila; Stubbs, G.T.; and Ashley, L.F., eds. *Only Connect: Readings on Children's Literature.* Toronto: Oxford University Press, 1980.

Elkind, David. *The Hurried Child.* Don Mills, Ont.: Addison- Wesley Publishers, 1988.

Estés, Clarissa Pinkola. *Women Who Run with the Wolves: Myths and Stories of the Wild Woman Archetype.* New York: Ballantine Books, 1992.

Fiske, John. *Reading the Popular.* London: Routledge, 1989.

Fiske, John. *Understanding Popular Culture.* London: Routledge, 1989.

Fowke, Edith. *Sally Go Round the Sun: 300 Songs, Rhymes and Games of Canadian Children.* Toronto: McClelland and Stewart, 1969.

Gilligan, Carol. *In a Different Voice: Psychological Theory and Women's Development.* Cambridge, Mass.: Harvard University Press, 1982.

Gilligan, Carol, and Brown, Lynn Mikel. *Meeting at the Crossroads: Women's Pyschology and Girls' Development.* Cambridge, Mass.: Harvard University Press, 1992.

Greer, Germaine. *Sex and Destiny: The Politics of Human Fertility.* London: Secker and Warburg, 1984.

Harmetz, Aljean. *The Making of the Wizard of Oz.* New York: Delta Books, 1977.

Heilbrun, Carolyn G. *Hamlet's Mother and Other Women.* New York: Columbia University Press, 1990.

Kinder, Marsha. *Playing with Power in Movies, Television and Video Games.* Berkeley, Calif.: University of California Press, 1991.

Lurie, Alison. *Don't Tell the Grown-ups: Subversive Children's Literature.* Boston: Little, Brown and Co., 1990.

Miller, Alice. *Banished Knowledge: Facing Childhood Injuries.* New York: Doubleday, 1990.

Miller, Alice. *Thou Shalt Not Be Aware: Society's Betrayal of the Child.* New York: New American Library, 1984.

Montagu, Ashley. *Growing Young.* New York: McGraw-Hill, 1981.

Opie, Iona, and Opie, Peter. *The Singing Game.* New York: Oxford University Press, 1985.

Paley, Vivian Gussin. *Boys and Girls: Superheroes in the Doll Corner.* Chicago: University of Chicago Press, 1984.

Reidelbach, Maria. *Completely Mad: A History of the Comic Book and Magazine.* Boston: Little, Brown and Co., 1991.

Rovin, Jeff. *The Illustrated Encyclopedia of Cartoon Animals.* New York: Prentice-Hall, 1991.

Singer, Dorothy G., and Singer, Jerome L. *The House of Make-Believe: Play and the Developing Imagination.* Cambridge, Mass.: Harvard University Press, 1990.

von Franz, Marie-Louise. *The Feminine in Fairytales.* Dallas, Texas: Spring Publications, 1972.

Wolfenstein, Martha. *Children's Humor.* Glencoe, Ill.: The Free Press, 1954.

Index

OTHER BOOKS FROM SECOND STORY PRESS